Wilfred E Buckley

HOW TO GET INTO
POLITICS

THE ART OF WINNING ELECTIONS

HOW TO GET INTO
POLITICS
THE ART OF WINNING ELECTIONS

BY

OLIVER CARLSON
Public and Industrial Relations
Counsellor, of the firm of
Northey & Carlson

AND

ALDRICH BLAKE
Political Research and
Organization Advisor

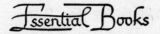

DUELL, SLOAN & PEARCE · NEW YORK

Dedicated
to
THE POLITICIAN
Symbol and Mirror
of
American Democracy

CONTENTS

CONTENTS

HOW TO GET INTO
POLITICS

THE ART OF WINNING ELECTIONS

Chapter I

IT MIGHT HAPPEN TO YOU

Once having attained legal voting age, every American citizen is a potential politician until the day of his death. There is no telling when personal ambition, espousal of a cause, or pressure from friends or business associates will catapult him into the political arena.

That American citizen might well be you.

In fact, it takes a huge army each year to fill the multitude of elective and appointive offices which constitute the cornerstone of our democracy. To this multitude of office seekers must be added the hundreds of thousands who serve on the various precinct, ward, city, county, Congressional, State and national committees which comprise the backbone of the American political party system.

Nor must we forget that there are the even greater number who though not running for office will nevertheless participate in our great political drama in one way or another. Some will make financial contributions; others will be called upon to deliver speeches for or against candidates or issues.

IMPORTANT LITTLE PEOPLE

This book was conceived and written to describe the lesser known but nonetheless potent factors which determine elections and influence the democratic process. We are going to tell something about the important little people, and how they manage to get along in that part of the political world about which the average citizen has such limited information.

The daily press tells little of the minute processes of politics. The handbooks of political parties are hardly more revealing. Text books in political science usually by-pass the technique and procedure of winning elections. They discuss, instead, programs, issues and personalities. Biographies of the more successful politicians and statesmen occasionally are very revealing and describe the more sensational methods by which their subjects have climbed to fame. But for the most part, until now, personal experience, guess work, or rule of thumb procedure have been the crude instruments by which the freshman politician charted his course and steered his craft in the dangerous waters of public opinion. No wonder then that the political mortality rate has been so high and that so few people really understand the underlying forces which give democracy its color.

PUBLIC RELATIONS OF POLITICS

We are making the embryonic politician our center-piece. Through his eyes we shall look out upon the people whose confidence and votes he hopes to win. With him we shall try to figure out what makes the politician tick and what makes the public react to him the way it does. Step by step we shall try to learn something about the politician, the party to which he belongs, the innocent bystanders known as the people, political organization in general, the precinct workers, finances, the public rostrum, propaganda and publicity, overall strategy and other factors pertaining to his public relations program which can make or break his political career, either during the campaign or after he is elected.

Naturally, the first step is to understand the rules of the political game and those who play it. It is an old, old game, as old as history itself. Let us begin, therefore, by briefly looking at the picture of American political life as it existed in the early days of the American republic and compare it with the picture we now see.

Chapter II

POLITICS—YESTERDAY AND TODAY

IN THE early decades of the American republic, politics was a profession. As in ancient Greece, men sought place, not a meal ticket. The elite of mind and fortune hungered for an opportunity to display their talents in the political arena. Every State capital from Bangor, Maine, to Atlanta, Georgia, as well as the national capital, was a cultural, social and intellectual center where gathered the literati, artists, musicians and social bigwigs to attend the legislative sessions and enjoy the mental combat.

In those days, a political debate was an event, whether held in the halls of Congress or in the public square of the backwoods town. People came for miles over almost impassable roads and made a week of it. The taverns were crowded with the eager participants of the young democracy. The cracker box was the rostrum for acrimonious discussion among local partisans on the issues of the day. There were few voters who had not seen or met the candidates for important State and national offices. Campaigns were highly personalized affairs—intellectual duels between the principals—with the voters acting as seconds.

There were few newspapers. The professional publicity agent was unknown. The modern pressure group had not yet appeared. Business was in its infancy. The functions of government were limited. There were no radio commentators to stimulate or befuddle the public mind. Public issues were comparatively few and simple.

From necessity, the politician was his own public relations expert even though the phrase "public relations" was unknown to him. He had to learn for himself the devious tricks of the trade, and he rose or fell in public esteem depending largely upon the power of his own personality and how wisely he used his native talents. Such advice as he received usually came from a few personal friends. Most of his decisions and actions were of his own making.

The relatively few people who voted had to think for themselves. Suffrage was still limited to the male population. The propertyless citizen could not vote. In 1788, when New York State ratified the Federal Constitution it was the only one of the thirteen original States which permitted all of the white male inhabitants above the age of twenty-one years to vote. Yet in that spirited election only 2869 votes were cast in New York

county, and 760 votes in Boston. In his *Economic
Origins of Jeffersonian Democracy,* Charles Beard estimated that less than 15,000 Pennsylvanians voted in the
ratification elections. In the first Congressional elections
3.6% of Maryland's white population participated. In
Massachusetts it amounted to 3% and in James Madi-
son's district in Virginia, to only 27%.

The public relations problem of the politician was
a simple one. His publics consisted of the large and
small landowners, and a few struggling merchants and
manufacturers scattered along the Atlantic seaboard.
The United States was nearly fifty years old before the
property qualification had been removed by the States.
Not until then did the new century of politics begin.

It is a curious and meaningful phenomenon that
Andrew Jackson, the first president elected by universal
white male suffrage, was the last of the line of America's
early statesmen who brought so much distinction to the
young republic. It almost seems as if night closed in on
American statesmanship with the passing of Jackson.
Now and then a great figure like Lincoln flashed across
the sky like a brilliant meteor, but gone were the
Washingtons, Jeffersons, Hamiltons, Marshalls, Jays,
Adamses, Monroes, Madisons, Henrys, Franklins, Otises,
Morrises, Randolphs, Clintons, Livingstons, Pinkneys
and the many others who had started the new nation
on its pilgrimage to wealth, power and fame—a galaxy
of names still known to every American school child

and more and more honored as the republic marches on.

Our early American statesmen have been generally recognized as among the greatest the world has ever known. But even in their day, politics had its unsavory side, with its demagogues and selfish, scheming men. By and large, however, there was in political life a certain patriotic and intellectual fervor which gradually declined with the rise of Jacksonianism and the spoils system under the impact of a vastly increased voting citizenship. The age of political chivalry had passed. The era of the common man had begun. Public relations in politics took on a new and difficult role.

Today, politics is all dressed up in a brand new garb. Personal political duelism is as obsolete as the old Model T. The politician, if he is half way smart, and can afford the luxury, is no longer his own public relations expert. He calls in a whole flock of propaganda and organization technicians, each supposedly a specialist in his own field. His publics are as varied as the complex civilization in which he lives. The politician must be "built up." He must establish his "pipe lines" into the inner sanctum of almost every conceivable type of club, society, lodge, church, trade union, business and other association or group. He must organize from the grass roots up.

To have a seat at the political table costs money—lots

of money. The problem of finances is nightmarish. Instead of selling himself, the politician usually must be sold. To a very large extent, he must let others do his thinking and make his decisions for him.

The people are as confused as the politicians. To think for themselves amid all the din is a futile gesture. The governmental waters constantly grow muddier. Even the Quiz Kids cannot keep up with all of the alphabetical agencies and their overlapping functions. The racial issue may pop up in any community, or along comes a picket line, the bootlegger, Ham'n Eggs, the sales tax, isolationism, lend-lease, communism, the Ku Klux Klan and an endless number of hopelessly snarled spools of political thread, which puzzle the politician as much as they do his publics. Now that women vote, the politician must look his best. Sex appeal counts. The poor as well as the rich crowd the polling booth. Ways must be found to satisfy both.

POLITICS AND BUSINESS

The primary object of the commercial world is to get in the black and stay there. In politics, the basic desire is to win elections. The tally sheets on which the votes are recorded are the ledgers which reveal profit or loss. The voting booth is the cash register.

In business, a public relations policy that keeps the dollars rolling in to meet payrolls and provide continuous profits, is a good policy. It means that the confidence of the customer has been won and kept. In politics, a public relations program that piles up the largest vote year after year, is a good program. It means that the good will of the voter has been earned and sustained.

Here our simile ends. General Motors may earn one dollar more in its fiscal year than the Ford Company, yet both may have enjoyed profitable seasons. The cash register may have been kind to each.

In politics there is no such devout consummation at the end of a gruelling campaign. A single vote, cast perhaps by some half-wit, is enough to plunge either Democrat or Republican into bankruptcy. Dividends for one or the other cease. Victory for one side or the other is total. The vanquished must begin life over again.

It has been said, and with great truth, that politics is a fickle thing, the most precarious business on earth. The cynic probably will suggest that this is because it is the worst managed human institution. The politician knows differently. He knows that the science of government, with all of its social, economic and political implications, is the most difficult of all the sciences. He knows that the job of wooing an electorate, and then keeping the chains of wedlock from breaking, is one of the most complex of all the problems in human behavior. He knows that the intangible products he has for sale cannot be advertised and sold like so many shoes, automobiles or cosmetics. He knows that managing the public business, which is everybody's business, is a far more intricate operation than keeping a private concern out of the red. In short, he knows that politics is dubbed the "worst managed" of man's affairs because the critic does not understand that its managerial requirements are the hardest to fill, and its problems the toughest to solve.

Chapter III

THE POLITICIAN

A GOOD many persons who think they want to follow a political career discover later that they have neither a liking for politics nor for the politician who manages politics. They get out of politics after a painful and often financially unprofitable experience.

What kind of a chap is this fellow we call a politician? What is his nature? What are his habits? Is he the sort you or I would want coming to our homes at all hours of the day and night?

The editor of a large metropolitan daily paper, after personally reporting the legislative session of a southwestern State, was asked what he thought of the politicians he had met.

"Well," he drawled, in his best southern accent, "they are the smartest, most energetic, most lovable sons of guns I have ever known."

Later, when this incident was related to a United States Senator, he dryly remarked that he thought the editor had greatly over-appraised his new political friends.

WHAT IS THE POLITICIAN LIKE?

In the mind of the public "all politicians are the same." They are regarded as a distinct class apart from the general citizenry. Actually, however, the politician is Mr. Average Citizen, the composite American, who reflects the common faults and virtues of the people.

Lawyers, doctors, engineers, teachers, ministers and others must procure a college degree or certificate before being allowed to engage in their professions. To that extent, they are distinguished from the man in the street. The skilled mechanic must have served his apprenticeship before he is allowed to operate a complicated machine. Business executives seldom are chosen unless they have had previous experience and training for the job assigned to them.

In politics, it is different. Any citizen may toss his hat in the ring for any job. If the hat looks good, he will be chosen regardless of whether or not he has a college degree, or has had previous training and experience in law-making or the administration of government. If a popular actor is elected to Congress, it simply means that the people are movie minded. If the sympathetic corner groceryman, who may not know a city ordinance from a charter provision, is elevated to the city council, it simply means that the people have the small merchant's complex. The actor and grocer may rise to the highest pinnacle of statescraft, but that does not alter the rule that the general level of democratic society cannot rise above the average virtue and intelligence of the people.

From this it should not be presumed that politicians as a class do not possess their own peculiarities of character. On the debit side, it may be said that they are an intensely suspicious, jealous, gossipy, impecunious and timorous lot. Behind a certain ego there is frequently concealed an inferiority complex. On the credit side, the politician is usually more tolerant, generous and better natured than those who sneer at him. In morals, intelligence, ability and integrity he measures up well with his fellow citizen, perhaps rates a little higher. His good undoubtedly exceed his bad qualities. Unless this were true, the democratic experiment in America could not have succeeded.

The politician is simply the finished product of the democratic factory which the people themselves operate and manage. If the time ever comes when the factory no longer pays dividends, the blame should not be placed on the product, but on those responsible for directing the policy of the plant—the people.

HIS INFERIORITY COMPLEX

Some of the faults and virtues of the politician stem from the unique environment in which he moves; others are inherent. They comprise a curious blend. Like the Russian peasant, the politician is a suspicious creature because he is constantly repressed. He is never quite welcome, for instance, in "polite society," never quite "accepted." He is seldom among the invited guests at the social functions of the upper crust. Now and then a politician is asked to join a service club, but politics and politicians are usually taboo at the noon day luncheon of the "leading citizens" of the community.

Inwardly, the politician feels that he does not "belong," and he becomes suspicious and envious of those who hold themselves aloof. He does not like to be called "a politician." He instinctively realizes that this is intended as a term of reproach indicating the low esteem in which he is held by the public generally. Accustomed to being snubbed in the drawing room, and often the victim of jibes in the public press, he seeks solace in a certain bravado which is apt to culminate in a sense of personal inflation.

It is not by accident that the politician is as jealous as the bride who sees her husband at the theater with another woman. The ambitions of the politician are not exactly modest. Once he has a meal ticket, the politician grasps less for money than for power. Always, there is someone standing in his way, a little above him. The seniority rule does not apply in politics. The politician goes up by pushing someone else down. He is jealous of those who occupy the brighter spots in the political sun. He froths when he sees the other fellow's name in the headlines. Politicians, like the Gods, demand exclusive worship, and they are constitutionally apprehensive of being displaced or outrun by their rivals. In his relations with others, the politician proceeds on the theory that "if you ain't fer me, you're agin me."

HOW HONEST IS THE POLITICIAN?

Contrary to what many people believe, politicians are not a pack of thieves. The national Congress has been singularly free from money scandals. Cases of bribery and embezzlement are extremely rare in the public service. In local and State affairs the record is not so good, but it is far from disgraceful.

Individual conduct always has its evil moments. Business and professional men often "cut corners" and do things which in public life would terminate their careers. The politician, let us remember, works under the glaring searchlights of a suspicious and skeptical public. His enemies never cease prying into his public record and private personal affairs. The public is apt to speak of politics as "dirty" because every day is wash day. The linen is in plain view.

Perhaps the politician deserves no credit for being a little more honest and circumspect than many of his fellow men. With him, it is a question of survival. The playboy who sneaks out with another girl without any qualm or conscience, is shocked when a politician gets caught. The people seem to have one set of moral standards for themselves, another for politicians.

THE POLITICIAN AS A "SPENDTHRIFT"

Most politicians lack money sense. Perhaps that is why they become politicians. Abraham Lincoln could not make a go of his little store, yet rose to the heights.

The names of big business men and industrial leaders are conspicuous by their absence on the list of famous American statesmen. The politician may understand the principles which underly successful trade and commerce without having the slightest idea about how to run a factory or store. Contrariwise, there is no assurance that the Fords and Wanamakers would make distinguished United States Senators or good Presidents.

Actually, the politician is more loose and careless in his money transactions than he is dishonest. He will borrow a dollar from another politician with no thought of paying it back, and he will lend a dollar just as quickly without expectation of asking for its return. Political notes are slow notes. They are seldom bankable paper.

Those who are in the habit of writing checks on the taxpayer's account are inclined to be careless about their own balances. Furthermore, politicians are naturally generous quite apart from the fact that they are accustomed to spending other people's money. They have to be, to sit in the game. They will buy a ticket for almost anything, and nonchalantly give and spend beyond their means. A hundred politicians leave the political arena as poor or poorer than when they entered, to every one that accumulates a fortune. The people observe the limousine, but fail to count the number of politicians afoot after long years of devotion to the public service.

THE POLITICAL TATTLER

One of the worst habits of the politician is his consuming appetite for gossip. He is a veritable genius at spreading tales, whether true or false. If the supply of gossip runs low, the politician brews a batch of his own. Mr. Harding has Negro blood in his veins; the governor was seen at a cafe with his secretary. The more vicious the yarn, the more a certain type of author chuckles, and the prouder he is of his fancied "political sagacity." Malicious political gossip has destroyed many an honest and forthright political career.

The conference room secrets always leak. The politician has a mania for wanting to let his friends "in on the know." It gives him a sense of importance. If a public relations man wants the "low down" all he need do is exchange "confidences" with the politician over a cup of coffee or glass of beer.

THE ART OF TRIMMING

Among the immense throng of politicians there are few who display the courage and fine independence which once distinguished American political life. There are many Henry Clays, few Grover Clevelands.

The modern politician has learned to trim his sails. He knows how to pull his punches. He is skilled in intrigue and compromise and seldom resorts to manly candor and bold expression. He will fight a personal political duel with an enemy, with no weapons barred, but in his relations with the people, he is timid and cowardly. His career and livelihood are at stake. He respects the overwhelming might of pressure groups and wisely gets out of their way.

When a tornado is seen in the sky the prudent citizen takes to the cellar, no matter how courageous he may be. The politician acts in precisely the same manner when he sees pressure groups furiously approaching him from all points of the political compass.

The complexity of the new politics does not contribute to that enviable display of public courage which the people claim to admire, but which they suffocate when they divide into special groups, each striving for its own selfish advantage and each possessed of enormous political power. The politician does the only thing he can do to survive the storm. He ducks, dodges, squirms and twists. Should he speak out and stand firm on the facts and his convictions, his name probably will be among the missing when the next political list is announced. Audacity sometimes brings cheers instead of jeers, but among politicians there are few who will dare the experiment.

ODD HABITS AND MANNERS

Politicians have extraordinary memories; they know what to forget and what to remember. They are as adept at ignoring a situation where they have "stuck their foot in it," trusting that the clamor will die out and not be revived, as they are at keeping alive a grudge against someone who has betrayed or maliciously injured them. The worst political enemies will crawl into bed together, but for different reasons. One may get under the bed clothes because some great principle of government is at stake; the other may only seek revenge for some fancied wrong. The "double cross" in politics is as poisonous as the venom of the viper; the political hatchet, when artfully applied, as deadly as the sting of a rattler.

In the uppermost political circles and in the lowest party councils, the habits of the politician, both good and bad, remain the same. Even the United States Senate is not immune from the faults and virtues of the politician. Commenting on the temperament of that august body in his *The Education of Henry Adams,* the author said:

"Although the Senate is much given to admiring in its members a superiority less obvious or quite invisible to outsiders, one Senator seldom proclaims his own inferiority to another, and still more seldom likes to be told of it."

The politician may have failed to "make his million while the going was good," but he has learned how "to put the votes in the ballot box," and to capitalize on the results. The cash register may jingle with the silver coins, but business men dance to the tune of politicians. The politician may be poor but he is no dullard. His knowledge is not acquired in pre-digested capsule form as so often is true of those who attend the widely advertised noon-day luncheon of some civic group. The politician does a lot of thinking for himself. He long ago learned not to rely too much on what he read in the newspapers. Whatever faults he may have, gullibility is not one of them.

Because he comes in contact with all religious shades, and people of every race and nationality, he is more inclined to be tolerant and mellow in his personal relationships and feelings. He does not go about with a sour look on his face or a cross word on his lips. He takes people as he finds them and tries to like them because he wants them to like him. A smile, handshake and pleasant good morning belong to his stock of goods. These he has drawn from the common stock of the buoyant, good natured American people of which he is a part.

Also, the politician is a marvel of energy like most of the men and women who have made America great by their unflagging toil and zest to do things. As one law maker remarked to his constituents:

"In the legislature, we work an eight hour shift— eight hours in the morning and eight hours at night."

It is never too early and never too late to give the politician a ring.

And, finally, with all of the sham and nonsense which typifies political activity, there are always moments when the politician feels those deep emotions, and experiences that high patriotic fervor, without which democratic virtue, which is love of country, could not exist.

Chapter IV

THE PARTY

IT WAS the fervent hope of most of the Founding Fathers that the government they worked so hard to establish would be able to function without the "curse of political parties."

But the very struggle for ratification of the Constitution gave rise to the first American political parties— the Federalists and anti-Federalists. Ever since this early period, parties have played a major role in the political life of the nation.

Now and then a politician has risen to national fame without attempting to establish intimate relations with any political party. But the George Norrises, the La-Guardias and La Follettes are unique and merely serve to demonstrate more fully the general rule which the vast majority of all politicians follow—steadfast loyalty to the party organization.

Detailed knowledge of political party machinery and

how it functions is a third condition precedent to a successful political career. Most of the public relations work of the politician is done through the various party committees. He reaches his wider public—the people themselves—through the party channels.

Writing a half century ago, James Bryce, in his American Commonwealth, said:

"The details of party organization have more to do with government than the Constitution."

In America, political parties march on, but with feebler step. Politicians are more numerous than ever, but they are an unhappier lot. Introduction of the nonpartisan idea into local government has torn great gaps in the party walls. Civil service has devoured most of the food upon which the politician has fed in the past. Famine now threatens the loyal party worker who still expects a job. Were it not for the new agencies which have grown out of the war and depression, starvation already would have been general in the party ranks. Still more civil service regulations blanket the hundreds of thousands of men and women who watch over the newly created bureaus and departments. The remaining party worker who wearily oils and greases the party machinery may yet have to strike for better party living conditions. Loss of all incentive to continue to do the party chores may cause him to seek other outlets for his enormous energy. The average party worker quits cold when all hope of reward is gone. Enthusiasm for the democratic ideal, or for party victory, is not an adequate substitute for bread and butter.

MAGNITUDE OF PARTY

But the political party has not lost all of its vigor as is evidenced by the number of men and women still eager and willing to do the party chores. In 1940, in the 48 states, there were 127,245 election precincts, or districts, in the great majority of which precinct committees, created either by statutory law or by voluntary act, existed. The number of party workers who occupied these coveted committee seats probably was not less than half a million. Perhaps a great many more. At least twice this number sought place in this, the smallest party unit, but were denied.

Upwards of another 250,000 party workers comprised the county committees in the 3070 counties of the nation. Other thousands graced the city, Congressional and State committee tables, with a few hundred fortunate enough to sit in the national councils as members of the national committees of the several parties. If, in addition, we include all of the members of the ward and other special committees, it is safe to estimate that not less than two million people play a consistently active role in political party affairs. This ignores the several million office holders who, though forbidden a seat at the party table by reason of civil service rules, and silenced by Hatch bills, big and little, nevertheless manage to bootleg their ideas, plans and orders to those who may still be articulate and who may still brew their political mash in the open.

These two million men and women are the insects which make coral islands grow. It is they who attend to the details of party organization, more important to government than the Constitution, according to Bryce.

When the public looks in the direction of the political party, it should look twice. If the first impression is that of a seething nest of annoying insects, the second will reveal that the party is merely a glorified, highly organized faction of the American people which can be dealt with collectively the same as a chamber of commerce, labor union or any other pressure group, by those who have relations with it. In short, the political party is just another "crowd," with all of the faults and virtues of the "crowd mind."

The major political parties happen to be the biggest crowds, and their concern is exclusively with politics and government.

THE POLITICAL SPRINGBOARD

For a prospective candidate for public office, or a citizen who desires to exercise political power indirectly, it is best to begin public activities by attending the precinct caucus, and party convention, whether local, State or national. A candidate must learn "what's cooking" and how it is cooked. He must know his fellow politician. He must acquire the essential habits of legality and formality which are a part of practical democracy in action.

His first glimpse into the maze of political party ramifications and intrigues, will not be as inspiring as he anticipates. He is certain to discover many little things which are not found in the political texts. Probably, he will many times wonder that democracy works at all!

In sum, the political party is simply organized politics. It is the principal instrumentality which provides the politician with a springboard from which to launch his flight into those places where power, fame and glory await his arrival.

The business man who seeks good public relations with his competitors joins his trade association or chamber of commerce. The worker who cherishes the respect and friendship of his fellow worker joins the union where his shop is unionized. The citizen who craves the sympathy of those who are religiously inspired, joins the church. The politician who is ambitious, and who is conscious of his public relations problem, joins a political party and preaches its gospel.

For the politician to attend his party precinct caucus is quite as important as for the business man to attend his noon-day luncheon, the worker his union meeting, the Baptist his Wednesday night prayer service.

The beginning of good public relations in politics is as simple as that!

Chapter V

THE PEOPLE

THERE is the classic story of Phocian, the Athenian statesman. When he was unexpectedly applauded by the people, he remarked:

"What have I done amiss!"

Measured by the standards of the modern American politician, Phocian had done nothing amiss. His public relations were excellent. He had won his audience.

But just who are the people? In the early decades of the American Republic, only free holders were "the people." By the thirties of the 19th century, the white, male propertyless citizens had joined the honored ranks. Constitutionally, at least, in the eighteen sixties the black man was admitted to the charmed circle. At the close of World War I, American femininity was included as a part of "the people." Late in 1943, the State of Georgia decreed that 18 year old boys and girls should also have the right to vote.

Gradually, the image of "the people" has broadened. Now it has been broken into many new images. The mind of the lowly politician is fatigued as it seeks to fathom and understand the big and little compartments and cells into which the twentieth century electorate is dividing itself. His back is bent under the staggering weight of his new and larger publics.

As always, there are the upper, middle and lower economic groups to contend with, as well as reactionary, conservative, liberal, radical and "red" political classifications to please. But to these have now been added the church vote, the veterans' vote, the labor vote, the farm vote, the business vote, the foreign vote, the Catholic vote, the Jewish vote, the women's vote, the youth vote, each of which, in turn, is subdivided into two or more factions. Then there are the votes of a growing number of smaller special groups likewise inclined to place their own separate problems and aims ahead of the general public welfare, and whose various shades and tempers make successful public relations in politics an intricate, complex, dizzying and extremely delicate affair.

Writing of American democracy in the 1830's, De Tocqueville, the brilliant French scholar, predicted that "if ever free (American) institutions are destroyed, that event may be attributed to the omnipotence of the majority, which may drive the minority to desperation."

Recent observers of contemporary political happenings, particularly in our law making bodies, now are beginning to ask whether American democracy may not be destroyed by the mass pressure of minority groups into which the electorate is rapidly dividing itself. It was easy, as Raymond Clapper pointed out, to control lobbying when it was confined to a handful of special interests. But how is democracy to control the privileged many—the half million miners, the numerous cattle growers, the railroad workers, the powerful farm and labor groups, the pension bloc, the hundreds of thousands of business men working through their national organizations?

There is even considerable prospect that some of the larger of these blocs, accustomed in the past to work within the framework of the two major political parties, may form parties of their own. The United States might thus be confronted with the same perils which destroyed France, Germany and some other European powers where the fragmentation of political parties precipitated a chaotic era in governmental activities.

The politician still may need to learn many lessons in public relations, but one of them is not how to remain on friendly terms with these powerful and grasping factions which have pre-empted the political pastures in which once browsed the general voting public. With few exceptions, he simply gives way to that combination of special group interests which he believes has the money and the power to re-elect him, seeking some compromise where possible but submitting to the terms of unconditional surrender when necessary to his own self preservation.

It is a curious anomaly that the people seem about to abdicate their throne in the political kingdom at the precise moment when the suffrage privilege is free to nearly everyone. The Noble Experiment of a quarter of a century ago did something more than send the liquor industry into temporary retirement. It opened the flood gates of minority rule by its startling example of how much can be accomplished by a few when properly organized, and when the few know how to apply the pressure.

Politics, political parties, politicians and the new hydra-headed electorate known as the people are the elements within the political kingdom around which the public relations battle for individual success, party and group advantage, and the survival of democratic government, is ceaselessly waged.

What are the latest weapons used by the antagonists and how are they wielded?

Chapter VI

THE POLITICIAN AND ORGANIZATION

ONE of the common characteristics of so many men and women who compete for public office is their complete auto-hypnotism and failure to comprehend the forces and factors which may point unerringly to their political defeat.

In their normal walks of life these citizens study market reports, consumer trends, batting averages, bank balances and weather forecasts—but once they have been bitten by the political bug they toss overboard all caution, and refuse to credit any reports which they do not like.

The candidate can see rosy hopes in a situation which would dismay him in any other aspect of life. He is unmoved by the arguments of his friends, the tears of his wife, or the warnings of his manager.

If he has tossed his hat in the ring, his first, and perhaps most difficult feat, is to throw off this auto-hypnotism and organize himself. Indeed, how can he expect to direct others intelligently unless he has first controlled himself?

Overconfidence is one of the most dangerous pitfalls.

It is well to remember that three words, "Rum, Rome and Rebellion," uttered by the Reverend Samuel Burchard a few days before the Presidential election of 1884, cost James G. Blaine, the Republican nominee, the prize which had been firmly within his grasp until then.

Anything can happen in politics and about everything does happen!

Proper organization is one of the important elements which the cocksure candidate often neglects or ignores. He imagines that his platform, or personality, or the magic of his name, will be enough to stampede the electorate.

Notwithstanding its importance, political organization seems to have become a neglected, almost a lost, art, except in the machine ruled cities where political organizations feed out of the political pop bottle. To be sure, some political leaders know what should be done, but unfortunately they fail to learn how to do it, or lack the proper tools with which to work.

PARTY ORGANIZATION

What are some of the principal difficulties which present themselves in political organization? What general organization patterns fit best into the party scheme? What are some of the organization problems the individual candidate should mull over before he launches his campaign?

Political campaigns are usually treated as seasonal affairs. The tent is pitched hastily. The American political party has not yet discovered the means by which it may provide itself with a steady and adequate income. It lives largely by promiscuously passing the hat. The turnover in party leaders and workers is enormous. New issues are constantly arising, requiring new strategy and new alignments. Except where the political boss has taken over, there is apt to be divided leadership and authority. Political committees seldom have research facilities of their own, and keep few permanent records. Political parties are not anchored to the ownership of property. They are renters and often make poor tenants. The hope of future reward is substituted for a salary check so far as most of the workers are concerned.

TYPES OF ORGANIZATION

Political organization falls into three general categories:

1. Arbitrary management with arbitrary control.
2. Democratic management with democratic control.
3. Arbitrary management with democratic control.

The first of these classifications has been largely appropriated by private industry. Corporate management is consistently arbitrary. Theoretically there is democratic control because the stockholders are given a vote, but actually control also is arbitrary, at least in big industry. Voting is mostly done by proxy and management controls the proxies. It is an arrangement ideally suited to private enterprise which is under no compulsion to observe the democratic process, but its application to the public business would mean political dictatorship.

Political bosses, who are dictators in their limited domains, make effective use of this type of organization, as do many candidates who have been long in the public service and who have created their own personal political machines which often operate with much greater smoothness than the squeaky party contrivance provided a few weeks or months before election.

√ Democratic management with democratic control is the usual pattern of political organization. This is one of the reasons that political organization on the whole is so ineffective. What is everybody's business is nobody's business. Whenever a committee is appointed to do a job which a single competent leader should do, the results may be tabulated in advance as poor. There is nothing quite so discouraging as laying out a program and then seeing someone rise to a "pint" of order and declare that it is "undemocratic" because the rank and file is not going to administer it. There is, indeed, nothing quite so fatal to the democratic process as the democratic managerial bug.

The third technique, arbitrary management with democratic control, is ideally suited to political party organization. Unfortunately, however, it is never tried. The rank and file have not yet learned to trust their leaders with adequate power and authority. They are not satisfied to wait for the periodic interval when they may quite properly step in and exercise democratic control by passing upon the general results of their leadership. They must have their say on every tiny detail of party policy and administration. Those who have the capacity to manage must either run the risk of being displaced or yield to the whims of those who haven't the slightest idea of what the responsibilities of leadership involve.

Political parties must make up their minds to give leadership a chance. Democratic control should only be exercised after leadership has had a fair opportunity to demonstrate its capacity.

"Campaigns are won between elections," is an old adage which, like so many others, is always being quoted by the politically wise men, but seldom heeded. Rather, from the usual lack of a plan and the frantic last minute efforts to produce some sort of order out of the campaign chaos, one would suppose that the parties and candidates imagine campaigns are won at the big rally the night before the voting instead of in the interval between elections.

The candidate who has first organized himself knows

that his exact plan of organization must vary with the size and complexion of the district in which the voting takes place, but he will have a plan. He knows that the enterprising manufacturer does not wait until the last moment to blueprint his sales program before placing a new product on the market; that long in advance he arranges his finances, studies his markets, trains his sales crew, prepares his publicity and advertising. Nothing is left to chance. Everything is ready when the sale of the product is announced.

Unfortunately, the candidate for political office is handicapped in many ways and is obliged to leave some things to chance. If, for instance, the wheels of the party organization creak, there is little he can do about it. But he can, if he knows how, and thinks about it, quickly make a much better political salesman out of the party worker. He can supplement the feeble aid which often is all that the party can give him, by creating a plan of his own based upon a thorough knowledge of political technique, organization and strategy. He can, at least, sit down and think his problems through.

Political budgets, workshops containing the proper tools, precinct workers and committees, the arrangement of meetings, preparation and delivery of speeches, campaign literature and platforms, timing—all of these and still other factors enter into a well integrated program of political organization and strategy.

The candidate who has intelligently blueprinted his work table and time sheet will discover that his public relations job has been greatly simplified and that his chances of election have been vastly improved.

He has at least organized himself.

Politics, like war, has its imponderables. The best organized armies are powerless to overcome the unforeseen intangibles of war and the best organized political campaign cannot overcome the flare-ups, crusades and political tides which so often spring up suddenly and unexpectedly.

No politician has yet devised a formula for sealing the lips or controlling the actions of any citizen who chooses to "shoot his mouth off." There is no way that the candidate can protect himself against the Reverend Burchards, no orthodox organization scheme which will overcome a political crusade or stop a tide which is running against him or his party.

Occasionally, it is possible to isolate and defeat a crusade by quickly organizing a counter crusade, largely through publicity and propaganda, but once a general political tide sets in, there is nothing for the candidate to do. For all who have not joined the tide, campaign strategy and organization are rendered worthless.

Ham 'n Eggs and the Townsend pension movements are examples of crusades which were successfully isolated and checked by the simple device of scaring a sufficient number of taxpayers into uniting for their defeat.

But the October 1929 panic, and subsequent events which sealed the doom of Mr. Hoover, constituted a tremendous political tidal wave which left a powerful Republican political organization impotent.

Crusades are usually positive in character; the crusaders seek some fancied benefit for themselves. On the other hand, tides are a negative reaction to some real or fancied abuse. The people are out to "get somebody." Again, the political crusade resembles the religious revival. Its enthusiasm cannot be maintained for long and many of the converted soon backslide.

One of the anomalies of politics is the tendency of the politician to neglect organization at times when it would be most effective, and to attempt it when organization is futile.

In politics as in war, "too little and too late" spells only defeat.

The foresighted candidate who finds himself unable to go along with the tide, either because of conviction or because he happens to be in the political party which is being swept out of office, does not waste time, energy and money but quietly takes shelter, waiting for the storm to pass.

Chapter VII

THE BUDGET

IN POLITICS, money doesn't just talk. It screams!

Men have been elected to public office without money. Parties also have been known to succeed when the party till was all but empty. Miracles do happen in politics and Lady Luck has been known to play a hand. The rules may be temporarily upset, but the game doesn't change. It is still necessary to put a nickel in the slot before the operator will answer. Too loud a jingle may cause bad public relations, but if there is no jingle at all there are apt to be no public relations.

One may only guess at the total cost of the thousands of separate campaigns which take place in a single election year. Official reports of contributions and expenditures required under a bizarre assortment of corrupt practices acts, do not begin to tell the story.

In 1940, for instance, the Democratic National Committee reported expenditures of $2,634,154. Mr. Roosevelt received approximately one vote for each penny expended. The cost per vote received by Mr. Willkie was only slightly more. On the basis of the total number of eligible voters in the nation, each of the two major political parties spent only a little more than a third of a cent per voter, according to the official figures. But instead of spending five million dollars between them, it is more likely that the Democrats and Republicans together spent from fifty to one hundred million dollars on the Presidential candidates alone. This was done in part through thousands of local and State committees or specially delegated agents, and in part indirectly through personal appeals to enthusiastic friends who were induced to underwrite many of the accounts which never appeared on the books. There is no way of telling how many other items were paid for by Tom, Dick and Harry who are forever hiring halls, getting out handbills, paying for lunches, buying the drinks and generally making themselves useful, or a nuisance.

The biennial cost of electing some six or seven thousand members of the State legislative bodies is not small change either. Including the primary campaigns, there are at least 25,000 candidates for these poorly rewarded posts. The very modest expenditure of five hundred dollars each would run the total bill to twelve and one-half million dollars. A candidate for Congress who can go through a primary and general election on five thousand dollars is a financial genius and public relations expert of the highest order. There are 435 Congressmen. But the number of candidates is invariably three or four times that many. If, on an average, each spent a mere $2,500, the bill would exceed five millions. United States Senatorships come much higher; governors are expensive campaign luxuries. These plums bring black market prices. The whole basket costs perhaps two or three million dollars. In addition, there are thousands of candidates for mayor, city councilman, school board, the judiciary, and for the minor township, city, county and state offices, each of whom requires a campaign fund. In off years the national expenditures may fall to as low as fifty of sixty millions. In Presidential election years the sum may amount to a quarter of a billion dollars. The political public relations budget is big business even in these days of astronomical figures.

BUDGET HARDSHIPS

This huge sum, difficult to raise, is seldom budgeted. Usually it is carelessly and wastefully spent. Party bills, and deficits left for individual candidates to pay, are accepted commonplaces in political finances. The managers and candidates have no time during the election hilarity to worry about the hangover. Besides, if the candidate wins, there are nearly always good natured people who will pay the deficit. Many generous givers prefer to wait until the campaign is over before making any donations. They prefer to help pay the deficit of the winner than to contribute to a candidate who may lose. These are the sure-shot players in politics.

At the beginning of a new fiscal year, the well regulated business appropriates a suitable amount for advertising and other costs involving its public relations program for the ensuing annual period. No such approach to sound budgeting and planning is possible in politics, except on those rare occasions when a candidate is able and willing to underwrite his own campaign. Or when there is an "angel" who will do it for him. In most instances, neither the political party nor the candidate knows how much money will be available. Nevertheless, it is highly important to prepare a detailed budget indicating the amount required for a well organized campaign, yet sufficiently flexible so that the less important items will be the ones stricken if the campaign fund falls below expectations. Obviously, if there must be curtailment, it is essential for the candidate to know where to reduce with the least injury to the general plan and strategy of the campaign.

FIRST CONSIDERATIONS

Preparation of the campaign budget not only is one of the basic preliminary steps in establishing satisfactory public relations with the voter; it also presents a difficult problem in political judgment, particularly for the individual candidate who must run the gauntlet of both a primary and general election, and, therefore, has the task of preparing not one, but two budgets. Some of the decisions he must make in advance of his public relations activities, involve the following situations:

1. He must gauge the political tide. If it is running heavily in the wrong direction, he might as well save his money and offer only token resistance. His nomination may serve the party in the sense that the place will not be vacant on the ticket, but it will have no other value. On the other hand, if the tide is strong and favorable, nomination may be equivalent to election. In that event he should spend without stint in the primary. If the signs point to a close election, he must decide whether to "shoot the works" in the primary and take a chance that additional funds will be available in the finals, or whether to keep part of his resources in reserve, and, if so, how much.

2. If it is a non-partisan primary where the law provides for a run-off between the two highest candidates, he must carefully calculate the possibility of getting a majority of the votes in the primary, making a run-off unnecessary. If the chances seem good, the candidate should spend his bankroll. If he is uncertain, it is best to hold back at least a portion of his funds for the general election. Or it may be that he should spend relatively more in the primary in order to win whatever

psychological advantage accrues from leading the ticket in the preliminary heat and looking like a winner in the finals.

3. If the candidate lives in a doubtful district or State, he should consider his chances of receiving financial support from the party treasury in case he is nominated. Advance inquiries should be made as to the amount of such support that might be given, if any. Liberal deductions, however, should be allowed, no matter what the assurances. Party leaders constitutionally lean toward the optimistic viewpoint.

4. The attitude of the press and the prospect of other aid must be carefully weighed. Strong newspaper support helps to fatten a lean budget. Radio programs, sponsored by political and civic groups, on which the candidate is endorsed and regularly publicized, may be worth hundreds, even thousands of dollars. Indeed, such support may obviate the need of raising more than a nominal campaign fund.

None of these decisions involves any expenditure of funds. On the contrary, they only require sound political judgment based upon a careful survey of the political forces and currents which may affect the election. No political realist finally makes up his mind to become a candidate until he has satisfied himself that the political omens are favorable and that there is reasonable hope of making the campaign ends meet, unless he is willing to "sacrifice himself" either for the party or some "cause" which he places above his own personal ambitions.

The conscience of the candidate must still wrestle with two problems involving political ethics and morals before he completes his budget:

1. What shall be his attitude toward the corrupt practices act which limits the amount of money he or his officially designated campaign committee may legally spend?
2. From what sources may he receive campaign contributions without compromising his freedom of action?

CORRUPT PRACTICES

In politics, as well as in every field of human relationship, there is the long as well as the short view. The temptation to do what is necessary in order to win the first trench is difficult to resist. It is so easy to alibi one's-self into believing that the wrong will not be repeated. Men in public life consistently chloroform their consciences, and do whatever must be done to prolong their political careers. Such men often die in government service, but their names are not recorded in the history books alongside those of the nation's great.

Federal law limits the expenditures of the national committee of each political party to three million dollars in a single campaign. The cost of mailing a letter to each of the sixty odd million voters in the nation is nearly two million dollars in postage alone, if sent first class. A Congressman may not legally spend more than $1,000 in his final campaign. A Congressional district averages about 160,000 voters. If sent first class, a letter addressed to each voter requires $4,800 in postage alone. A legislative district may contain as many as forty thousand voters. A letter to each voter will require $1,200 in three cent stamps—as much, probably, as the annual salary of a member of the legislative body.

Obviously, under the present system, most political money must be bootlegged, or the democratic election process would all but cease. There would be no such thing as public relations in politics. To circumvent the law, the candidate is obliged to operate through trustees, confidential agents and "This Advertisement Paid For by Friends" committees, which are supposed to be volunteer groups acting apart from the official campaign and moved entirely by altruistic and patriotic motives.

The whole ghastly farce is comparable only to the prohibition era, except that the effects of bootlegged political money are even worse than those of bootlegged whiskey. It is perfectly plain that the very foundations of democratic government are undermined when elections are paid for by resort to hypocritical subterfuge and phony bookkeeping records.

HOW THE PEOPLE REACT

The candidate who skirts the law need not fear that his relations with the people will be injured so long as he confines his expenditures to legitimate campaign practices. The people want to be informed. They know that it costs money—a great deal more than the law allows. They seek the arguments and facts; dote on the thrills and frills of politics. Their common sense tells them when a candidate is spending beyond the bounds of public decency, and they rebel. Once they discover that large sums of money are being used to purchase "influence" and to debauch the electorate, instead of for legitimate propaganda and electioneering purposes, punishment is certain. The day of judgment may be long deferred, but it is sure to come.

Spending money in a campaign to inform the voters so that they may reach an intelligent decision is one way, perhaps the best way, to strengthen the democratic process. To prevent such spending, if it were possible to do so, would destroy democratic government which is based upon enlightened public opinion. The people understand this better than the purists. They will not quarrel with a candidate who spends legitimately and who does not compromise himself by soliciting and passing debased political bootleg money.

THE MONEY BAGS

It is not the corrupt practices act which need discourage generous campaign budgeting, nor suggest an obstacle to confident and dependable relations with the voting public. The money bags themselves, as well as the knowledge of where they are kept and who stands guard, are the matters which will weigh heavily on the candidate who has a political conscience and who desires to establish mutual respect between himself and his public on a permanent basis.

Where are these money bags and how much do they contain?

One is filled with copper, another with nickel, a third with silver, and a fourth with gold. An odd bag, heavier than the rest, contains the precious jewels of politics. The coppers come from the public; the nickels from the candidate's personal friends; the silver pieces from those who hate—the people with a grudge; the gold mostly from selfish, designing persons and groups, and the jewels from that rare and precious creature known as an "angel." Most candidates like their copper, nickel, silver, gold and diamonds well mixed.

In the matter of raising his budget, the incumbent candidate usually has an enormous advantage. He has been able to do many favors, big and small, for persons and groups. He knows where the money bags are and about how much they will yield. The chances are good that he will receive some aggressive newspaper support. His organization is more or less ready made. He can begin his campaign later than his opponents. Indeed, he probably has been campaigning during all of the time that he has held public office. Because of these advantages he will risk relatively more of his personal funds. The incumbent enjoys the banker's percentage in the game.

The challengers must throw out their lines much earlier. No matter how well they think they know the district, the incumbent is apt to be more up to date in his information. Political arrangements have an uncanny way of changing rapidly. New faces and new forces are always appearing. Old money bags are emptied, new ones take their place. One never quite retreads the same public relations path in politics.

POLITICAL SMALL CHANGE

In general, the public gives penuriously to political candidates and causes. The people have been educated and disciplined in the matter of contributing to charitable and other worthy private enterprises. They have yet to learn what it means to support those activities which so vitally affect their democratic way of life. Political parties have failed completely in their most important public relations job—that of educating the average voter to the need and duty of backing his political convictions with his pocketbook. The politically minded chip in their mite if properly solicited, but the average citizen feels that he has done enough if he takes the trouble to vote. No party or candidate relies on popular donations to finance a campaign. Perhaps five percent of the budget can be raised by opening the bag of coppers which the people so zealously guard.

Personal friends of the candidates seldom respond generously. A few five and ten spots may be pried loose. Now and then someone gives a little more. Occasionally a hundred dollars, or even two hundred is dropped in the till. The candidate who raises as much as ten percent of his budget from among his more intimate acquaintances has done extremely well. The nickels extracted from personal friends go farther than the coppers, but it takes a lot of both to provide an adequate campaign fund.

Except in campaigns for major offices such as governor, or the United States Senate, where large sums of money are required, the candidate himself should be prepared to underwrite at least fifteen percent of his campaign budget. The canvass may not go as well as expected so he should have a little something of his own to tide over the financial crises which are so common and painful in politics. With fifteen percent of his budget in hand and another fifteen percent reasonably certain from small contributions, the candidate can at least count on being able to do the absolutely essential things.

The silver bags in politics are held by those who hate. Sometimes these bags are sufficient to provide the entire campaign budget. An incumbent councilman may have failed to keep his promise to vote for a zoning ordinance affecting a piece of property; a member of the State legislature may have forgotten his pledge to support a bill sponsored by a wealthy sportsman whose hobby is the protection of wild game from the indiscriminate killer; a Congressman may have overlooked his agreement to recommend a friend for the postmaster's job. The victims are angry, hurt. They are waiting for a chance to get even. They are eager to write their checks and to prevail on others to do likewise, if they think the opposition candidate has a fair chance to win. They want nothing in return. Revenge can be one of the sweetest things in life.

THE BIGGER MONEY

It requires no divining rod to discover where the bags of gold are located. Most of them are in the cellars of those who have dollars and cents business with government. The contractor, real estate operator, business and industry in general, and sometimes the underworld, hold the golden purse strings which can provide a large campaign budget. Some of this gold is now stached in the store rooms of the farm and labor organizations. Almost any candidate who shows promise of being the victor can have his share of this gold. To give to both sides, provided each has a fair chance to win, is a common practice in politics. There is nothing like playing a sure thing.

Much of this gold is untainted. Many business men as well as farm and labor groups give generously to political candidates and causes out of a patriotic desire to improve government. On the other hand there exists what politicians call "dirty money." It circulates more freely in local and State campaigns where local contractors and others have a direct stake in the result. Here organized vice is apt to take a hand. Gamblers for instance do not pay out without expecting the payoff.

It is astonishing how often the reform crowd furnishes the candidate with the votes while the gamblers put up the money to make him the winner. After the election, it is usually discovered that the gamblers, not the churches, knew their man. Where bargains are made involving juicy returns if the candidate is successful, the amount of dirty money may run into thousands of dollars even in a campaign for one of the lesser offices like city councilman, and many times that much if a district or prosecuting attorney's job is the prize.

Finally, there is the gold that is neither pure nor entirely without taint. Most business men have an instinctive fear of politics and politicians. Many of them simply want to be let alone. They write generous checks hoping that they will escape the horrors of half-baked legislation and the annoyances of political blackmail.

Their contributions in reality are simply insurance premiums against the unwarranted political attacks which industry has learned to expect, and, sometimes by its conduct, has invited.

Here public relations are delicate. No element of hatred or patriotic motive inspires the giver. No specific promise is wanted or exacted. Nevertheless the implication is plain; the candidate is expected to "be fair," and to be fair usually means that in these cases he is no longer quite free. If he is unwilling to assist his benefactor, he is at least supposed not to do anything which will injure his interests. Occasionally, the circumstances are such that as a public official he can remain true to his own ideals and at the same time he can help those who helped him.

One of the oddest phenomena of politics is the carefree manner in which otherwise cautious business men give to political campaigns. They seldom inquire what the money is to be used for, and almost never ask to see the budget figures. If they were invited to invest a similar amount in a private venture, these same business men would investigate the management and finances of the project before making up their minds. But in politics it seems to be the habit to ask no questions. The check is drawn, or the cash is paid over, usually to a third party, and the transaction is closed. Often the candidate never even knows of the contribution. The money simply disappears. Some day, perhaps, a law will be passed to protect the gullible business man from being fooled and robbed by the lowly politician. Business men would save a great deal of money if they saw to it that their contributions were used to pay certain specified items in the campaign budget. A few have discovered this secret of making their dollars count.

Alone, in his bejeweled throne room, sits the political angel. To find one of these rare creatures is like searching for the holy grail. Sometimes our angel is a kindly old man who wants to help a friend. Maybe he is a social climber who is ambitious that his wife stand at the head of the receiving line at the Governor's reception. Again he may be an aggressive young man who is willing to open his gem box because he believes in the cause the candidate has championed; or perhaps our angel is one of those strange female creatures whose emotions and interests are inexplicable.

To find and sell an angel on the holy duty of financing a political campaign is one of the most artful jobs in the whole mysterious category of public relations. No promises are exacted of the lucky candidate. His principal problem is to keep his angel veiled. For angels have been known to divide or transfer their affections for reasons as obscure as the motives which inspired them to open their jewel bags in the first instance.

Money is seldom easy to get in politics. In the preliminary heat, it is especially scarce. Many contributors want to see the horses run before they place their bets. This subjects the conscience of the candidate to additional strains. He knows that he must qualify in the primary or return to the stables, perhaps for a permanent rest. Promises which may later lead to serious embarrassment in his relations with the people, often are made when the pressure mounts and seems unbearable.

FINANCING THE PARTY

Actually, there is no real excuse why either of the major political parties should be without adequate funds to carry on their legitimate business. Properly organized, the precinct, county and State committeemen alone could provide the money for the ordinary party needs.

In 1940, there were approximately 130,000 precinct or election districts in the United States. Technically, each precinct committee should have consisted of at least five members (some States had as many as seven, others none), making a total of 650,000 precinct committeemen for each of the two major political parties if fully organized. There were 3,070 counties. The number of county committeemen (theoretically) was not less than fifty for each county, or 153,500 in all. There were 48 States averaging 100 state committeemen each (probably more), making a total of not less than 4,800 committeemen serving the several State organizations.

As a condition precedent for membership on these committees, suppose that each precinct committeeman were compelled under the party constitution to pay twenty-five cents a month, or three dollars a year into the party treasury; each county committeeman fifty cents a month, or six dollars, and each State committeeman one dollar a month, or twelve dollars a year. In that event each major party treasury would be enriched annually as follows:

```
650,000 precinct committeemen, $3 each....$1,950,000
 15,350 county committeemen, $6 each....       92,100
  4,800 State committeemen, $12 each......      57,600
                                             ──────────
                    TOTAL............$2,099,700
```

Now, let us assume that each precinct committeeman was expected to raise at least another three dollars in his precinct in small amounts, that each county committeeman was responsible for procuring an extra ten dollar bill, and each State committeeman another twenty-five dollars. These contributions would amount to an additional $2,223,500 each year.

In short, the grand total of monies raised annually in this manner for each of the major parties would be $4,323,200, or more than $90,000 for each State if equally divided.

APPORTIONMENT OF FUNDS

Obviously every penny of this money should be paid into the national party treasury, to be re-allocated to the States in proportion to their population or needs, after the national committee has first deducted such amount as might be essential to its own budget. In turn, the States should be left free to allot whatever portion of their funds they saw fit to the several county committees, making due allowance, of course, for the size and requirements of the various areas served.

It is true that the amounts thus allocated to the States and counties would vary enormously. Connecticut, for instance, with only 169 election districts (the least number of any of the states in 1940) undoubtedly would be entitled to receive more money than it had contributed. On the other hand, California, with the most number of precincts (13,692 in 1940) probably could get along on less. Only the national committees of the parties would be in close enough touch with the overall political outlook to decide intelligently exactly where the dollars should go.

Chapter VIII

SPENDING CAMPAIGN FUNDS

No TWO campaign budgets are ever the same, but all bear certain common resemblances. Few people, including many politicians, have the slightest idea of the legitimate requirements of a candidate who seeks even a comparatively small office. What may be in reality a modest public relations budget often is mistaken for a slush fund. For example, the budget of a candidate for a seat in the State legislature may seem like an extravagance, almost a scandal, yet actually every item is legitimate, and essential to a well rounded program designed to reach and inform the voters. Such a budget, suggested here for the purposes of illustration, might be considerably expanded without in any manner corrupting the democratic process.

Our imaginary district is located within a great metropolitan area. It contains four distinct communities, each served by a local weekly. There is one labor paper and there are two small local group organs. The district contains forty thousand registered voters and one hundred seventy-five precincts. There are no local radio stations and no daily papers except those which circulate throughout the metropolitan area. These latter cannot be depended upon to give the campaign more than an occasional paragraph in their political columns. The political factions are about evenly divided. It promises to be a normal campaign, with no tides running. There is a chance to defeat the incumbent, who will not lack for money. Our budget, estimated for the primary election alone, contains the following items arranged by groups in the order of their importance so that pruning may be done intelligently if reductions become necessary.

1. Miscellaneous & Reserve Fund	$ 300.00	
2. Literature & Campaign Cards	150.00	
3. Precinct Workers	500.00	
4. Precinct Manager	150.00	
	$1,100.00	$1,100.00
5. Adv. Four Community Papers	$ 640.00	
6. Adv. Labor & Group Organs	160.00	
	$ 800.00	800.00
7. Bill Boards	$ 500.00	500.00
8. Letterheads, Envelopes & Postage	$ 200.00	
9. Two Stenographers @ $100 each	200.00	
10. One Radio Program, Major Station	200.00	
	$ 600.00	600.00

11. Distribution of Literature ....$ 100.00
12. Rent of Four Headquarters, $25 each 100.00
13. Four Headquarters Managers, $50 each 200.00
14. Bumper Signs for Cars 50.00
15. Quarter Cards 50.00

$ 500.00   500.00

Total Budget $3,500.00

THE PRUNING PROCESS

This budget, in order to nominate a candidate for the State legislature whose members receive only a few hundred dollars a year as compensation, may seem extravagant to the average citizen. To the candidate who must conduct the campaign, it will seem too little. No provision is made for a professional publicity agent, or for polls which reflect public sentiment, for fact finding and for many of the corollaries which help to make public relations in politics a success. Actually, the budget provides for the expenditure of slightly less than nine cents on each of the forty thousand voters who reside in the district. An extra five hundred dollars, bringing the per capita expenditure to exactly ten cents, would greatly strengthen the budget and the candidate's chances of winning. The budget does contemplate modest compensation for those who take an active part in the campaign, but this should not shock the business man who is not exactly in the habit of relying on volunteer assistance to promote buying relations with his customers. The much heralded efficiency of business might suffer, too, if it dared not, or were unable, to spend the money essential to its successful conduct.

Quite obviously this budget does not conform to the corrupt practices limitation on campaign expenditures. Item one alone exceeds the maximum amount a candidate for the legislature may legally spend in most States. If the laws were literally enforced, in many instances a candidate actually would be prevented from printing and distributing enough campaign cards and leaflets to publicize his name and his platform properly, unless, perchance, Uncle Sam would give him free postage, or unless other methods of distribution were without cost.

How reasonable and legitimate the suggested budget actually is, and how well it conforms to the spirit and requirements of the democratic process will appear from a detailed examination of its contents.

If the candidate finds that he must lop $500 from his original budget estimates, it is best that he begin with items eleven to fifteen, at the bottom of the list. A display of quarter cards on telephone poles, fences and trees helps to impress the voter with the candidate's name and is worth something as institutional advertising. Comparatively few voters will place such cards in their windows. If used at all, the quarter card should be displayed late in the campaign; otherwise it becomes dirty and torn. Youngsters draw mustaches on the candidate's handsome lips, and the effect may be ludicrous. Often words are pencilled in, which are not exactly flattering.

Bumper signs on automobiles are in much the same category. They are a nuisance to the car owner and wind or rain are fatal to them. While they are good advertising because people's eyes are attracted to a sign on a moving vehicle, they are not essential to a candidate's success. Institutional advertising is as legitimate in politics as in business, but when the campaign budget is low, quarter cards and bumper signs are frills which may be relinquished without too much regret.

The first idea of most candidates is to open headquarters. They do not feel that they are "in business" until they have an office with a sign on the door. In our imaginary legislative district, there are four distinct communities; therefore, there must be four separate headquarters to satisfy everyone. Sometimes friends of the candidate will volunteer as managers, but it is best for the candidate to employ popular local political figures if he wants to be sure that the office doors will be kept open and that he will reap the maximum reward for this expenditure. An allowance of fifty dollars each for four managers who may spend as much as three or four weeks on the job, is hardly excessive. Actually, these forlorn looking places, called campaign headquarters, mostly serve as rendezvous where the political loafers and gossipers may congregate. The general public probably will notice the banner stretched across the doorway, but will not venture inside. The candidate's real workshop should be somewhere else, where his office staff will not be annoyed. The average campaign headquarters has a certain psychological value, but that is about all. It at least gives the appearance of a business-like campaign. It is always desirable in politics to keep up with the Joneses and the other candidates are pretty certain to be well housed if their budgets allow it. However, if the budget must be cut, the headquarters is an excellent place to begin in the relatively small local campaign.

To get his campaign leaflets into the hands of each voter is one of the worst problems a candidate with limited resources faces. To mail a single piece of litera-ture, at second class rates, to 40,000 voters, will cost $600 in postage alone. The waste is enormous. Many voters will have died or moved. Addressing the envelopes is expensive unless volunteers can be enlisted for that pur-pose. The more economical way is to have a distributing agency deliver the material to each of the approximately 17,000 homes in the district. But even this method of distribution is unsatisfactory. The housewife is apt to think the leaflet is just another circular advertising a quack doctor, so it goes either into the wastebasket or incinerator.

The candidate who must curtail may profitably strike the item of distribution from his budget and fall back on his precinct workers to do the job. Many voters will be missed but those who are personally handed the historic document may at least examine the cover page and read the candidate's name. Some may even read what the candidate has to say when sufficiently urged by the worker. If the candidate can afford it, the ideal arrangement is to have two pieces of literature, one to be distributed by a professional agency, the other to be personally delivered by the precinct worker. Our budget does not provide for any such extravagance.

THE GOING GETS TOUGHER

The budget has now been reduced to $3,000, but, unfortunately, further pruning is necessary. Items eight, nine and ten must now be considered by the candidate. He decides that he will have to be satisfied with one stenographer instead of two and that he will cut his printing bill and postage in half. With one assistant, and perhaps a little volunteer help, he can do most of the essential things in his workshop at home. He hesitates to cancel the one major broadcast which his budget has provided, but this is necessary. The cost of the broadcast is high, anyway, considering the number of voters who will be accidentally tuned in on the station he has chosen. The big stations do not have local rates. The candidate can ascertain in advance about how many listeners he will have who reside in the district by consulting one of the big down-town professional advertising agencies. He is almost certain to discover that the per capita cost of talking to each of the voters in his district who will be listening, is high. He reasons that a single broadcast is not enough to do much good, anyway, and to contract for a series of informative broadcasts in order to press home his points and attract a following, is far beyond his means. Reluctantly, the radio item is stricken, and the budget is now reduced to $2,600.

Bill boards come next. The candidate had definitely counted on at least a few of these. Secretly, he had hoped to see his name in big letters with perhaps a glorified picture of himself, on huge signs located at strategic street intersections in many parts of the district. The voters cannot fail to notice bill boards. The name of the candidate is constantly before them. If they have not taken much interest in the election, they will recall the big letters they saw when they mark their ballot. But the candidate hasn't the money, therefore no bill boards for him. The budget has now shrunk to $2,100. The campaign has really begun to suffer. The pinch is at hand. The candidate has lost most of the intangible elements of a well balanced public relations program.

He still clings desperately to items five and six comprising his newspaper advertising allowance. He knows that the little ads will not in themselves win him many votes, but he wants the good will of the editors. If he does no advertising in the community weeklies and in the small labor and group organs, he is afraid that his

news releases will be cut, perhaps relegated to an incon-
spicuous column and page, or that maybe they will be
ignored entirely. His advertising budget is extremely
small and he dislikes to reduce it. The political advertising rates, often double the commercial scale, average
about two dollars an inch. He has provided in his
budget for only three ads in each of the four community
weeklies, one of forty, and two of twenty inches each, in
three successive issues. He has a hunch that the incumbent candidate will take at least one full page ad in each
of these weeklies, and probably get the "break" in the
news columns. He has set aside a mere pittance in his
budget for the less generally read labor and group
organs. Again, however, the candidate has no choice
except to prune. He reduces item five by half and takes
another $100 from the amount he had expected to spend
in the smaller papers. His total budget is now reduced
to only $1,680.

Despair is in his heart. He has received a few coppers
and nickels, but the silver and jewel bags are still in hid-
ing. The candidate must cut some more. Perhaps he
should first search for gold. His conscience begins to act
up badly. His blood pressure rises. His wife is cross and
threatens to divorce him. No, she won't sign a mortgage
on the house, and the car belongs to her. The candidate
finally decides to cut again. He will get along without a
stenographer. He will write his own letters. He won't
order any campaign letterheads and envelopes. He

would like to continue with his reduced advertising budget, but the money simply isn't available. He slices his budget by another $580 and now it stands at $1,100.

IN BALANCE AT LAST

At long last it looks as if the candidate can make both ends meet. He has $500 of his own money which he has not spent if he planned wisely and prepared his budget in advance. This is almost exactly fifteen per cent of his original budget estimate. There is still reasonable hope that his personal acquaintances and new friends will contribute an additional fifteen per cent, making $1,000 in all. He can, in a squeeze, borrow a hundred dollars at the bank and preserve items one to four intact. With a good precinct organization he may still pull through. He will talk the poor man's language and try to create sympathy for himself. Others have won seats in the legislature with less than $1,100 to spend.

But there are more disappointments. The candidate finds it necessary to reduce his budget another $500. He clips $200 from his miscellaneous and emergency fund and decides to dispense with a precinct manager. He will organize and direct the precinct workers himself. The budget is finally in balance. It has been reduced from $3,500 to $750. There may still be a deficit but it will not be large. The candidate has sufficient money to pay for his campaign literature and cards, to employ one hundred precinct workers at five dollars each, and to take care of a few odd political sundries. His basic grass roots organization plan is still intact. He has sacrificed everything else to it.

It is amazing how much service an enthusiastic precinct worker will render for a five dollar bill. And the results of effective precinct organization are still more astonishing. The candidate still has a chance if he works the precincts properly. He has one hundred seventy-five precincts to canvass, but only one hundred workers. He should be able to enlist thirty or forty volunteers to cover a part of those precincts in which he cannot afford to hire anyone. He must cover some of the precincts himself. Every member of the organization must be inspired to do double duty.

THE "SNEAK" PLAY

Perhaps the candidate has no money of his own. He has no budget. Even so, he need not give up all hope if he has looked far enough ahead.

Many years ago a young man by the name of Carl Mapes ran for Congress in the Fifth Congressional District of Michigan. He was too smart to imagine that he could defeat the popular incumbent by the usual public relations methods used in politics. He decided on a "gum-shoe" campaign. Quietly he organized his youthful admirers into an army of gum-shoers. They were trained to put just one thought in the voter's mind:

"Carl has no chance, but he is a fine young man. With

a little seasoning he may go places. We do not want to see him humiliated by being overwhelmingly defeated. It might end a promising political career. Why not give him a complimentary vote?"

The "complimentary vote" sent Carl Mapes to Congress where he remained until he died thirty years later, the second oldest member of Congress in point of service.

Budget making for councilmanic, Congressional, gubernatorial and campaigns in other political units, is little different from that when a seat in the State legislature is the prize. The amount of money required will vary and the sources will not be the same. Some items, like radio and bill boards, for instance, will assume major importance. Precinct organization may be too expensive to undertake. The press cannot be ignored. Different branches of the budget tree will have to be pruned and other factors peculiar to the nature of the campaign taken into consideration, but the fundamental conception and technique will not change.

One would suppose that the permanent committees of the various political parties would show some perspective in the matter of budget preparation and financing, yet almost none do. Party affairs, like the affairs of individual candidates, nearly always are conducted on a catch-as-catch-can basis. Shop opens a few weeks before election and closes election night. The country either has been saved or it has gone to the dogs, depending upon which side has won. There wasn't any budget, but there is another deficit for the party managers to worry over.

There is one deep consoling thought for the candidate who is bedeviled by his budget nightmare and who wakes up in the night thinking about the money bags. The chances are that his opponents are suffering the same agonies and tortures. That may be one of the reasons why so many candidates who have done such a miserable public relations job, nevertheless come out ahead.

Somebody has to win.

Chapter IX

THE WORKSHOP

AN ADEQUATE workshop, as distinguished from a campaign headquarters, is one of the "musts" in sound political organization. Its size and nature of course will depend upon the size and nature of the political unit served.

In the metropolitan area, it is impossible to maintain the proper kind of a workshop without at least one regularly employed research and publicity expert. He should be selected purely on a professional basis. His job is to assemble the facts and to disseminate them according to the approved standards of his profession. He is not supposed to "run the party." In the small counties and cities, where public relations are less complex and where less data is required, it should be possible to find someone, fairly competent, to volunteer enough spare time to assemble the vital information and keep it up-to-date and ready for use. Public study clubs could be used as excellent feeders for this highly important task.

A businesslike workshop undoubtedly would attract financial support. People will contribute money to a project when they are convinced that it is worth an investment. Many a political committee is left starving because it has nothing to sell but "the cause." Men of affairs seldom are seen in the party workshop because it contains nothing but a second hand desk, an old wooden file and a few uncomfortable chairs. Where the workshop is combined with the campaign headquarters, as it usually is, no one with real business ventures in.

ESSENTIAL CAMPAIGN TOOLS

The political plant should be equipped with a high speed mimeograph, addressograph, typewriters, filing cabinets and all of the small gadgets which denote an efficient business office, and should have a comfortably furnished room for private consultation. Goods are not sold in barns. It should also contain a practical reference library and facilities for a modern publicity and fact finding service.

Without an adequate plant and the proper atmosphere, the public relations of the party are certain to be conducted on a hit and miss basis.

A good reference library will include the following:

1. *Directories:* General directories, postal and telephone directories of every community in the county; business and professional directories, and

a directory by street numbers as well as by names; Congressional, State legislative and newspaper directories.

2. *Lists:* Official registration lists of voters in each of the respective political units comprising the county; lists of all farm and labor organizations; Negro organizations, foreign groups and leaders; lists of available public meeting places with rental rates, capacity, location and time available; special lists of persons available for professional services, including a good cartoonist and popular entertainers; lists of possible and actual contributors, of public officials, leaders of pressure groups, teachers, doctors, lawyers, precinct workers, speakers, money raisers, organizers, clerical workers and others whose services may be of value. In short, a general political inventory of Who's Who in the civic and political domain.

3. *Books, Pamphlets, Clippings:* The World Almanac, Election laws, Bartlett's Famous Quotations, an up-to-date encyclopedia, campaign text books, political leaflets and pamphlets, a few standard works on political and economic problems, and, finally, elaborate scrap books containing items of interest about the principal political figures and issues.

4. *A Morgue:* Photographs, cuts and mats of prominent party leaders, with biographical sketches con-

taining detailed accounts of their public utterances and activities, including those of members of the opposition parties.

5. *Maps:* Maps of the county with information about all communities and roads; maps of each political unit, including the precinct; maps, properly colored, to show particular information as to the political, racial and occupational complexion of the various areas within the county; maps which reveal the social strata, industrial or economic interests of the several communities; maps showing the physical, social and psychological "geography" of the section in which good public relations must be established.

6. *Historical File:* Election results over a long period of time, not only as to candidates but pertaining to initiative and referendum measures, all of which reveal the voting tendencies of the community; apt quotes from national leaders of the past and present; oratorical embellishments from poets, statesmen and philosophers.

7. *Outline for Speeches:* Data on special subjects available to study clubs, churches, racial and national groups, and to those who may convey the message of the party through means of the public rostrum or radio.

8. *Information Bureau:* A record of reliable employ-

ment bureaus and all government agencies which render special services; a file of attorneys who are willing to serve in charitable cases; names of social and other workers who will assist those in difficulty; suggestions as to how to avoid red tape when dealing with a public agency. Such services win friends for the party.

VITAL SERVICES

Comparatively few candidates for public office are able to employ their own press agent, or maintain their own publicity and fact finding bureau. To many office seekers and persons engaged in promoting public causes, the simplest tactics of the press agent are a mystery (and an apparently insurmountable obstacle). Political parties of course cannot render special publicity services to every candidate and every cause but they can, and should, provide the guidance which will simplify the problem for others. Their publicity and fact finding service may at least enlighten the candidates upon many matters. It can include, for instance, the following tips and services, available to any party candidate for the asking:

1. The names, addresses and phone numbers of cartoonists, "ghost" writers, photographers, sign painters, distributors, printers and a list of the news-

papers and other periodicals, their political advertising rates, circulation, policies, "deadlines" and other material data.

2. The rates of radio stations, the number of listeners who will be tuned in on an average at any given period, relative cost of reaching the listeners for each station, and whether censorship of political script is strict or flexible.

3. "Layouts" for campaign literature, including the color scheme. Large business enterprises which spend millions of dollars for advertising copy have learned the value of proper layout and color effect. People are largely sold through their eyes.

4. Suggestions of material that will appeal to particular groups, or which should be avoided. It is easy to give offense in politics, hard to repair the damage. Before the candidate takes pen in hand or opens his mouth, it is important for him to know the whims and hobbies of particular groups, whether the pet cause be eugenics, gardens, court reform, tobacco, booze, religion, or cat hospitals.

5. Information about political reporters on local newspapers, news agencies and various channels through which news is disseminated.

6. General hints about the release of news, what is news, and how to "make news" that will find its way into print.

Except for the incumbents, most candidates begin their campaigns from scratch. They do not even know the boundary lines of the district which they hope to serve. They may have seen the name of the president of the Lion's Club in the local paper, but they have no idea as to who is head of Circle 3 of the Methodist Church. They have no "They Do" list—the names of people who get things done or who mold public opinion through the service group, the lodge, the labor union, the church, or by conversation between hands at the Wednesday night Bridge Club.

Often it takes the candidate many weeks to get his bearings. The time he spends trying to locate a precinct, getting hold of some special list, finding out who's who in the various sections of his district, making up his mind on the style of campaign leaflet he prefers and ascertaining how much it costs, learning where and at what hour the Navy Mothers meet, and on all of the other seemingly petty, yet highly important details of the campaign, is simply staggering.

Campaigns are of short duration. Hence, there is nothing quite so precious as time. If established, and properly stocked, a central political workshop set up by the party to serve all candidates could be a great time saver, and more, a bargain counter for the forlorn candidate whose resources are limited.

In view of the fact that the potentialities of a sound

public relations program in politics are so great, and the cost of setting up in business is so small, it is amazing that political leadership has failed to provide itself with an adequate supply of the tools needed to do a good job, or that no private agency has undertaken to assemble these tools and sell them at a profit.

Chapter X

THE PRECINCT

THE precinct is the mud sill of the political party structure, the base of its organization triangle. At its apex stands the national committee. The ward, city, county, Congressional and State committees are its sides.

Too many people who want to play the political game look with disdain upon the lowly precinct worker.

In the city and town, today's election precinct usually covers only a few blocks; in the rural area it may include several square miles, but it is still a neighborhood. The cracker box in the cross roads store still exists. The number of voters in the precinct varies from a scant half dozen in isolated mountain and desert regions to several hundred in the congested centers of the great metropolis. Roughly speaking, the precinct chairman has from three to four hundred voters in his tiny kingdom. But the average number of families that must be called on and convinced is seldom more than one hundred fifty.

In New York State there are approximately 10,000 election districts. A net shift of ten votes in each means a difference of 200,000 votes in favor of one party or the other, enough to win where the electorate is about equally divided. A clever precinct worker will get these extra ten votes, whether in New York State or elsewhere. No precinct worker should be sent into the field without training.* His public relations may do more harm than good if he does not understand the nature of his task and how to do it. Those ten votes are too precious to risk losing by the wrong kind of canvass.

PRECINCT PROBLEMS

Precinct work on behalf of Presidential, gubernatorial and United States Senatorial candidates is important, but it is still more effective in campaigns for the lesser offices. In the more intimate and usually less spectacular local campaign, the voter is more easily influenced. Often he does not care especially about the elec-

* In the presidential campaign of 1940, Dorothy McAllister, then head of the Women's Division of the Democratic National Committee, established Precinct Schools in West Virginia. These were the first of their kind and the idea caught hold quickly. Michigan and New York soon established similar schools. Workers travelled more than 100 miles in West Virginia to "attend class." According to the reports of these sessions, women came away with: (1) A clearer understanding of what sympathetic precinct organization can do in determining the outcome of elections; (2) a better realization of selecting efficient and alert officials; (3) new ways to use campaign literature; (4) new ways of getting this literature to the voters; (5) realization that visiting homes is the responsibility of women in pre-election activity; and (6) better conception of women's political responsibility.

tion and would not get to the polls but for persistent urging by the precinct worker.

It has been estimated that about twenty per cent of the voters have strictly independent opinions and leanings in any election involving party tickets. If there are three hundred voters in a precinct, this means that the problem of the precinct chairman is to discover and convince the sixty persons whose votes may be influenced. If it is a primary or non-partisan election, the percentage of voters who have no fixed prejudices or attachments is certain to be a great deal larger. For some of the minor offices as much as ninety per cent of the electorate may be totally indifferent. In this event, if one candidate has an effective precinct organization, and the others have none, his election is assured.

Where an effective precinct committee has been long established, its organization problem is greatly simplified. It will have the voters well catalogued. It will know who are the most effective workers and which voters always vote a straight party ticket as well as which are apt to stray from the party fold. Unless there is a political tide running, organization of the precinct is a matter of finding out which of the party members are a bit shaky, or disgruntled, and applying pressure on them. Of course, in addition, the independent voter and the wavering adherent of the opposition party, must be successfully wooed.

The precinct committee has five principal functions to perform:

1. To raise money.
2. To arrange at least one meeting in the precinct at which outside speakers are present.
3. To distribute the campaign literature properly and inform the voters about special broadcasts.
4. To canvass the voters who reside in the precinct.
5. To get out the vote.

FINANCES

The public relations budget of the precinct committee is small. In the average precinct of 300 voters as little as fifty dollars will suffice to do a reasonably good job. Twice that amount would constitute a "slush fund." The committee usually has neither the hundred nor the fifty dollars. Often it has exactly nothing.

If funds in the required amount were available, the budget would look something like this:

Two preliminary canvassers at $5 each for two days	$20.00
Handbills for precinct meeting	1.50
Hall and chairs	5.00
Form letter to voters	5.00
Boys to deliver letters	2.00
Two workers on election day, $5 each	10.00
Emergency & miscellaneous	6.50
Total	$50.00

Campaign literature is furnished free to the precinct committee by the central party headquarters, often in such quantity that much of it is wasted, and sometimes of a variety that more harm than good would result from its distribution. Cars that are used to get out the vote are almost always loaned and the only precinct headquarters is usually the home of some member of the precinct committee.

It would seem easy to raise fifty dollars in the precinct. One ten, four fives, and twenty one dollar bills, ought to be forthcoming out of 300 voters if the rules for raising popular funds in small amounts make sense. But nothing involving money in politics seems to make sense. The money relations are always bad.

People who contribute to political causes are surprisingly few. The politically minded citizen prefers to give to the county, State and particularly to the national committee, instead of to the precinct fund. He wants his name on one or more of the big name lists. He wants to be known to the "big shots" as a party contributor. Some day he may want to be postmaster or cock his feet on the governor's desk. A contribution to the precinct campaign will not give him the "in" which he wants.

Actually, there are always people in the precinct with a flare for raising money. The best vote getters, however, are seldom good money raisers, and the vote getters are more apt to accupy the seats on the precinct committee. Quite as often the skilled money raiser has no idea of how to present the party cause. The big problem is to bring the two together and make them work as a team.

There is an old campaign axiom which says "spend your money in the precinct." It might advantageously be changed to "get your money in the precinct." It is there to get but someone must ask for it and it must be the *right* someone. To send the wrong solicitor either will produce no results or will establish the worst kind of public relations; probably both. The drive for campaign money in the precinct should be organized with all of the skill and forethought of a drive for the Community Chest, and with the same earmarks of integrity.

A precinct committee should be both able and willing, if necessary, to underwrite at least a part of the campaign budget. Some money usually must be advanced before an intelligent drive for contributions can be launched, no matter what the nature of the cause. This is particularly true in politics because the solicitation must be restricted to those voters who are friendly, and it is impossible to determine which of them are favorable before the precinct canvass is undertaken. Occasionally, there is a precinct committee which has preserved the list of former contributors, making a start comparatively easy. This happens so rarely, however, that it may be dismissed as an odd and curious political phenomenon. The vast majority of precinct committees begin from scratch in each campaign, and end up by scratching for the few dollars with which to complete their public relations program.

Chapter XI

THE PRECINCT CAMPAIGN

THE first step in the precinct campaign is to probe the mind of the voter as to party loyalty as well as to his opinions on issues and candidates.

The precinct canvass is to politics what the inventory is to the merchant. The precinct committee must know the inner feelings of the voters before the campaign itself can be intelligently planned, much the same as the merchant must gauge the needs and whims of his customers before he will know in what respect to replenish his shelves for the new season.

For the preliminary canvass it is usually advisable to select someone only slightly known in the neighborhood, or perhaps, a skilled worker from some other precinct. The strategy is to catch the voter off guard. John Q. Citizen is a cagey animal. If he thinks someone is fishing for information, he will shut up like a clam. He is not above giving the worker a "bum steer." How he votes he considers to be strictly his own business.

Canvassing a precinct properly is an art. Intensive training is required. People are touchier about their politics than they are about their Fuller brushes. Few of the commercial rules of salesmanship apply.

The principal problem of the commercial house to house canvasser is to get inside the front door. The most ticklish problem of the precinct worker on his first call is to remain *outside* and conduct his public relations on the front porch. If he must step inside because the toast is burning or the baby squawking, he should politely refuse a chair if invited to sit down. Once he sits down, he may let himself in for an hour's harangue on the benefits of a vegetarian diet or the evils of wearing slacks. There are a lot of lonely people in the world who like to talk and tell their troubles. The time of the precinct worker is valuable. If he is caught in the pincers of an easy chair and a glib tongue, he may find it hard to escape without offending the voter. The rule works two ways. If the voter is politically wise, he will entertain an unsophisticated worker representing the candidate or party he does not favor for as long as possible. A cup of tea or glass of beer will help to prolong the stay. In one local campaign in Los Angeles, this technique, methodically planned, worked surprisingly well. The workers of the defeated candidate never did complete their canvass.

After the canvasser rings the bell, he should step back in the best Fuller style, particularly if he belongs to the male sex. Housewives are afraid of a man at the front door; and of bill collectors, whether men or women. The worker should have nothing visible to indicate his business. When the door is opened, he should withdraw slightly, then slowly move forward with a friendly smile. The stage is set for his public relations job.

PROBING THE VOTER'S MIND

The worker should not give his name, unless asked, nor any hint of the real nature of his business. To introduce himself, for example, as a member of the Democratic party committee may be fatal. Every Republican would freeze in his tracks. The independent voter won't be any too warm. It is sufficient if the canvasser inconspicuously produces a copy of the voter's registration list for the precinct, containing the names, addresses and party affiliations of the registrants.

"Just checking the voters' list, Mrs. Smith, to make sure you are registered right. I assume that you are Mrs. Smith. Oh, yes, that's fine. Let's see, you are registered as a Democrat. Correct? Thanks. From Indiana, by any chance?"

"Hoosier! I'll say not. I'm a Texas Democrat where they always vote 'er straight."

By now Mrs. Smith has the door half way open and

is peering over the shoulder of the worker to make sure she is correctly registered.

"Funny, I notice your husband—guess it's your husband—is a Republican, Mrs. Smith."

"Yes, from Maine. One of them black sheep. Ha! I'll kill his vote on election day. Never did know much about politics. And there's my son. Got him on your list? Sure, that's him right there on that line. Yes, he's a Democrat but one o' them wobbly kind. Got new-fangled ideas. Kinda independent about his votin'. It's discouragin' with me from Texas."

"Sure am sorry about the boy. I'm a Democrat, too. Always vote my ticket. Heard the committee is getting up a little fund to carry the precinct. Gotta beat those Republicans. I'm gonna give my dollar."

"Count me in, too. I'd give a buck any time to keep them Republicans out. And let me know if there's any meetin's."

The precinct worker hurries away. Only one member of the family, the son, needs a special call. The interview has not taken over three minutes. The fishing has been good.

But now let us suppose that it is a primary or non-partisan election and the worker is supporting a particular candidate. The approach and preliminary conversation are the same, then the technique changes.

"What you doin' this for now?" blurts Mrs. Smith. "There ain't no election. Election? Oh, yes, I forgot.

Gettin' pretty close, too. The old man ain't here and the boy works. Yes, you've got 'em down right on the list."

The trained precinct worker will start to leave, then, apparently as an afterthought, turn back.

"A lot o' people I see are knockin' Bill Blevins. Wonder why. He's runnin' for the legislature. Know anything about him, Mrs. Smith? I'm kinda curious."

Mrs. Smith perks up.

"Sure I heerd o' Blevins. The old man says he's for the unions and was seen in one of them there picket lines. People around here kinda gone against the unions. But that boy o' ours, we never do seem to git together. Heerd him say that Blevins was a good guy. Kinda think the kid joined the union. When did you say the election was? We never miss votin'!"

The technique of quickly probing the voter's mind, finding out who he is for and against, and why, without arousing his suspicions, is as simple as that.

It is easy for the precinct worker to spot the indifferent voter. He shows no interest, does no talking, and often appears sullen. Occasionally, he literally slams the door in the worker's face. Whoever reaches him last is most apt to control his vote. He should be seen early and often on election day or otherwise he may not get to the polls.

The really great enigma is the so-called doubtful voter. Although he may freely express his doubt, the worker never can be quite certain that he is not holding something back. If he asks for campaign literature, the chances are that he really has not made up his mind. He is extraordinarily canny about not committing himself. Perhaps he is just naturally wishy-washy, or he may be politically wise and slyly trying to work the worker. In short, the "doubtful" voter may be on an information hunt himself.

RECORDING THE INFORMATION

On the preliminary canvass, the worker should not distribute any campaign literature or cards. He is not seeking to make votes. He is simply trying to discover the real attitude of the voter. His only equipment, in addition to the registration list, should be the precinct cards with the names and addresses of the voters, all carefully concealed. These cards should not be arranged alphabetically but by streets, so that the worker may go up one side of the block and down the other without retracing his steps. If no one answers the bell, he should inquire at the next house about the habits of the absen-tee. In normal times, call-backs are comparatively few. They must be made by the worker on his own time; otherwise the expense of the preliminary canvass may exceed the budget for that purpose. Two workers should be able to canvass an average precinct in a couple of days, with a few loose ends to pick up later. Fast work-ers, who know something about the habits of the voters, have been known to make as many as twenty calls in a single hour.

As soon as the interview has been completed, and the voter is out of sight, the worker should note on the voter's card exactly what he has learned. For example, the initials "OK" may be used to signify that the voter is favorable; "NG" that he is beyond redemption; "D" that he is doubtful; "IND" that he is indifferent. The notation "Against Unions" is sufficient to indicate the prejudice that must be overcome if Mrs. Smith is to be lured into Candidate Blevin's camp. "Always votes" is a valuable bit of information; it saves work on election day. "Willing To Give" is the tip-off that here is a prospect for the precious dollar so essential in the precinct campaign. The worker should note carefully the names of those who have moved or are dead, or may have to be driven to the polls in a car because of illness. The names of new voters also should be recorded. With this information the labors of the precinct committee are greatly simplified.

The preliminary canvass should be undertaken about thirty days before election. To begin too early may mean that the preliminary canvass will not reveal the tendencies of the voters; to start too late may be fatal. This is a matter to be decided by the precinct committee whose business it is to watch and gauge the general trends of politics, particularly in the neighborhood.

Other means than the voters' registration list may be

used to attract the voter's attention and allay his suspicions. The neighborhood may be polled for any number of reasons. The conversational approach and technique is not always the same. Indeed, it probably will vary in every case, but the basic strategy remains. The canvass is a failure unless the voter is induced to reveal his inner feelings and opinions. Those who do not are the ones to watch. The battle centers around them.

It is easy to check the labors of the precinct worker after the cards are turned in. The precinct chairman need only contact three or four personal friends upon whom the worker was supposed to call. If he turns in a card for these voters, but failed to call on them, the fraud is apparent. If the information on the card is inaccurate, there is reason to distrust either the ability or loyalty of the worker. It is well to warn the workers that some of their calls will be checked.

Summarization of the data contained on the precinct cards will make it comparatively simple to plan an intelligent precinct campaign. The doubtful and indifferent voters must somehow be gotten out to the precinct meeting. Mrs. Smith, too, should be given a special invitation to attend for she is sure to give that dollar when donations for the precinct fund are requested. If the precinct has a complex against organized labor, campaign literature extolling the party's pro-labor attitude should not be distributed. The central headquarters should be advised to use such literature somewhere else.

THE FOLLOW-UP CALL

Arrangements must be made to have the right person make a special call on the doubtful and indifferent voters. The party leader who has a flare for raising money must be induced to canvass the loyal partisans who are able to give a few dollars to the campaign fund. In short, following the preliminary canvass, the campaign is on in earnest. There is a vital public relations job to do and it must be done well if the precinct is to be carried or the normal party vote increased.

The follow-up interview with the doubtful or indifferent voter should be undertaken by a volunteer either intimately acquainted with the voter, or by someone whose name is known and respected in the neighborhood. Big names count in the precinct as well as at the national capitol. It is difficult, usually impossible, to prevail on an outstanding citizen to spend the time necessary to make the preliminary canvass. This work should be paid for, particularly if the committee wants to be sure that the canvass will be completed. The job is not an easy one; the worker earns his money. The volunteer who may start the job with high enthusiasm is not apt to finish it. He is under no particular responsibility to do so. If a meeting of the Red Cross interferes, or he has a headache, the volunteer lays off. The paid worker, on the other hand, makes it his business to complete the canvass and collect his money as soon as possible.

Special calls require special talents and often the obscure precinct worker has neither the prestige nor the knowledge to convince the voter. If it becomes known that the worker is being paid for his services, his influence is diminished. Few voters will resent the modest compensation he has received for the precinct poll, but the average citizen resents "influence" that is paid for.

The easy chair will serve a good purpose on the follow-up call. The public relations job now has shifted from the front porch to the family circle. Again the indirect approach is usually best. The easiest way to overcome a voter's prejudice or sympathy is to create a new prejudice or sympathy. If convinced that he has been lied to, imposed upon, or that a candidate is being "persecuted," the voter is in the bag. His resentment sticks out all over him. Mr. and Mrs. Smith, who are inclined to be against Bill Blevins, might be approached something like this:

"Too bad about the strike at the plant, isn't it? No, I don't like strikes. They oughta be stopped. Still, I don't see how the boys can buy pork chops on those wages they get. After all, a man has to eat. Glad your son doesn't work there, Mrs. Smith. Hear about Bill Blevins? They say he joined the picket line. They're using it against him in the election. It may beat him. I kinda feel sorry for Bill. Good friend of mine. He's only doing what you and I'd probably be doing if we worked there. Just staying with his gang. Bill's loyal. Shows he'd stick with the common folks if he got elected. May be something to this union business after all. A guy that works at a machine for eight hours is entitled to eat good. I understand Bill's opponent is using this picket line affair against him. Strikes me as unfair. Hate to see anyone made the goat. Glad your boy doesn't work at that plant. If he did he'd probably be in the picket line too. Understand he joined the union. Fine boy. Would hate to see that used against *him* if he ever ran for the legislature. Maybe he will some day. Make a fine candidate. Hate to see Bill Blevins treated so unfair like."

If this kind of "reasoning" fails to weaken Mr. and Mrs. Smith, it would be just as well to mark them "NG," unless the son can be induced to use his influence. By all means, the son must be seen.

PSYCHOLOGICAL "TRICKS"

There are as many variations in this type of interview as there are voters interviewed. There are as many new "angles" developed as there are doubtful and indifferent voters in the precinct. It is as easy to lose a voter by one procedure as to win him by another. In the holy pursuit of the doubtful and indifferent voter, there are curious and illuminating episodes. One precinct worker who had diligently kept after a housewife, confidently pushed the doorbell for the last time.

"Heck, Mamma, here's that political woman again," shouted the little boy who answered the bell. Mamma, too, didn't like it. She was getting dinner. She did not go to the polls on election day.

Yet the same worker explained that she had often been rewarded for her persistency.

"You've worked so hard that I am going to vote for your candidate," she was told by a lady upon whom she had called many times. "I hadn't expected to vote that way, but I want you to win. You deserve success after all the hard work you have done."

Anything can happen in politics. Often the worker can win a vote by making the election a personal issue.

"Now really Mrs. Jones, you don't care very much who wins, but it means a lot to me. If I carry the precinct I expect to get a job and I need one badly."

The voter wilts. Among the strongest emotions of the people is human kindness. They like to do as well as receive little favors. One worker was taking a straw vote. A lady in a fashionable home peeked through the slit in the door, listened for a moment, and then made a deprecatory remark.

"Well, anyway, I'm just trying to make a living," quickly snapped the worker. "I'm paid a nickel for every straw vote I get, and I need the money. It's hard work, too, if you want to know it."

It was lunch time. The lady opened the door, dropped her ballot in the cigar box and gave the worker tea and sandwiches.

"You look so tired, dear," she said.

PRECINCT WORK ENJOYABLE

Properly conducted, the precinct canvass is the most effective work done in politics. It succeeds best in the middle class and industrial neighborhood. The precinct worker should avoid the big homes where they have maids. In such vicinities, the public relations job should be done by telephone and by someone who is extremely well regarded in the neighborhood.

Great discretion should be used in selecting the precinct workers. If the population of a neighborhood is predominantly pro-labor, the most effective public relations job will be done by a person known to be friendly to labor. In rural precincts much of the precinct work necessarily must be done at the pie supper, dance, farm meeting or in the country store. Where possible every home, nevertheless, should be canvassed. Even in the big machine-ruled metropolis, where precinct work is largely a matter of giving and taking orders, the battle of wits and skill goes on.

With all of its headaches, the precinct canvass also has its compensations. No worker should take himself or the election too seriously. He must fit himself to the mood of the voter, laugh with him and cry with him. In his rounds, he may be able to do some little favor that will win a lifelong friend and make the next campaign easier. Most voters are moved by small things. They are more interested in sports, gardening or stamp collecting than they are in who wins the election. The gift of an old baseball glove to the youngster may make friends of an entire family. To enjoy and influence neighbors, one must be neighborly. To be neighborly is the essence of good public relations in the precinct campaign. In the course of his canvass, the worker may even be lucky enough to meet his future wife.

There is one little chore that the precinct chairman must not overlook when the canvass is completed. He should pay the workers promptly and take a receipt in full. Otherwise, the neighborhood public relations may suddenly turn sour and remain so indefinitely. There is nothing quite so venomous in politics as the tongue of the worker who has done his job and finds himself unable to collect.

ELECTION DAY

The party precinct rally is the curtain raiser for election day. It should be staged about ten days before the voting.

Such political rallies primarily are designed to stimulate interest in the voting and not to convince the voter. Another principal purpose is to raise whatever funds may still be necessary to balance the campaign budget. If possible an outside speaker should be procured. People like to see a new face and hear a different voice, but local talent should not be ignored. There are prima donnas in neighborhoods as well as in Grand Opera. It is wise to give these prima donnas a role. If the hand-bills advertise "good eats" as well as the speaker, the crowd is apt to be much larger. It is easy to get dona-tions of food and drink for a neighborhood affair even when it is difficult to get money. Coffee and doughnuts have their own technique in stimulating the collection when the precinct chairman asks for money.

If there is a deficit in the campaign fund, the chair-man should state the amount. If additional funds are required, the amount should be revealed and the pur-pose for which the money is to be used, explained. It pays to be specific, particularly in politics where skepti-cism is a permanent state of mind. The mere suggestion that members of the precinct committee who "have worked day and night for the party," will have to pay the deficit if the meeting does not respond, is usually sufficient to bring a generous response. The voter does not want to seem cheap. He will give his mite. Even if the bills have been paid, but money is still needed for election day, he will open his purse. He has already been convinced that "victory is certain if the vote is out." Maybe he has bet a new hat on the outcome; he is not going to take any chances now. The battle must be won regardless of cost; the enemy routed and humili-ated.

Volunteers are called upon to do the few remaining precinct chores, the speakers urge everyone to be sure "to vote early and late," and the meeting ends with a rising vote of thanks to the guest who "sure told it to us straight." Another political rally is proclaimed a success, Probably not a vote was changed, but the workers and the crowd feel better. Once more they have paid homage to the sacred democratic process. And the precinct till is no longer empty!

GETTING OUT THE VOTE

The big moment for the merchant who has advertised his closing out sale for several weeks, is at nine o'clock on a Monday morning. The big moment for the precinct worker is when the polls open at six o'clock on a Tuesday morning. An hour previously a letter should have been quietly slipped under the front door of each home where the voters were known to be favorable, exhorting them to be sure to vote and thanking them for their support. This last campaign chore can be performed by reliable boys. In the case of individual candidates running for minor offices such last minute appeals, addressed to every voter in the precinct, may be enough to carry the precinct, even if no other work has been done. The letter should be signed by the right person and very carefully phrased. Often the apparently little things are big things in the minds of many voters who have no particular choice of candidates.

If the pre-election work has been well done, election day is a joy. Most of the hours are leisurely ones for the worker. But if the preliminaries have been neglected, the worker might as well stay home. Merely getting out the vote may do more harm than good. The problem is to make sure that only the favorable votes are cast.

In a normal election the procedure which the precinct worker should follow is simple. The only precinct cards which need concern him are those marked "OK" and "Indifferent." Inwardly, he hopes the opposition will forget to vote. He leaves the doubtful voter severely alone. Inquiry following elections too often has revealed that four-fifths of the so-called doubtful vote really favored the opposition. The doubtful voter is adept at showing his hand to the side he favors, concealing it from the other. The indifferent voter, on the other hand, must be seen early and reminded that it is election day. He may have to be called on several times before he can be persuaded to vote. It is better if the worker walks to the polls with him, or takes him in a car. The indifferent voter must be "poodle dogged." The last person with him is pretty apt to "vote him."

There is little for the worker to do on election day until after the first rush of voters in the early morning hours. After nine o'clock the voting slows up until noon. The worker's first job is to check the voting register to see who has already voted. He can now destroy many of his precinct cards. The worker's labors are reduced by the number of citizens who have already voted. Next he makes a preliminary tour of the precinct, on foot, if the precinct is not too large. A car is merely a nuisance. The favorable voters are reminded that it is election day and the worker asks them what time they intend to vote. He will not see them again unless the time has passed for them to appear at the polling place. In his preliminary round the worker also will offer to have the friendly voter taken to the polls in a car, if he prefers.

Each precinct worker should have at least one and perhaps two cars at his disposal during the day; more if the precinct is large in area. The worker does not use a car very often, but when he does need a car he needs it badly.

At regular intervals he rechecks the voters' register. Gradually the number of cards which require his attention dwindles until by late afternoon he may have only twenty-five or thirty left. Now he must really hustle. The time is short. He does not hesitate to break in on the evening meal. Every vote counts. It is surprising how many people will skip their dessert in order to vote if the precinct worker is there to remind them of their duty. At five minutes before closing time, the worker is still on the job—if he is conscientious. There is still time to get some listless or forgetful voter to the polls. If he has done his job well, perhaps twenty or more citizens have voted who might otherwise have stayed home. Twenty votes per election district in New York state adds 200,000 votes to the party's total. A few extra votes per precinct often are enough to turn the tide.

THE WRITE-IN CANDIDATE

In the rare so-called write-in campaign where the candidate does not have his name printed on the ballot, the technique on election day is entirely different. There are no leisure moments. The polls must be manned from the minute they open until they close. Where two election day workers can handle a precinct in an ordinary campaign, as many as ten or more are required in the write-in election.

As he approaches the polling booth, every voter must be handed a pencil to write with, and a slip showing the correct way to spell the candidate's name; otherwise he may forget to write the name in, or use the wrong initial or letter, thus spoiling the ballot under many State laws.

A few years ago the late "Doc" Brinkley, famous goat gland specialist, made a write-in campaign for governor of Kansas. He would have won if his name had not been spelled incorrectly so many times. His radio broadcasts convinced the people that he had been a martyr to the "persecutions" of the medical fraternity, but they failed to impress the memory of the voter sufficiently to enable him to spell the name correctly after he was in the voting booth. Fewer radio broadcasts and more precinct workers to man the polling places on election day might have changed the result.

There are tricks which may be used, not unfairly, to attract the attention of the voter who is about to enter the polling place. Most voters resent being handed a card or a piece of campaign literature at the last moment. It implies that they are about to exercise their sovereign right of suffrage without sufficient knowledge of the candidates and issues. Usually they stuff the printed matter in their pockets without looking at it, or throw it disgustedly on the sidewalk. They do not propose to be "told." Except in the write-in campaign, the precinct worker has no business electioneering at the polls. He has work to do elsewhere in the precinct. In the write-in campaign, however, he and his political aides must be on hand all of the time the polls are open.

Even so, the situation is a delicate one. Often the voter is in a hurry. He does not want to be stopped. He wants to cast his vote and get back to his business, or go home. The problem of the precinct worker is to distract his attention long enough to hand him the pencil and the slip of paper without offending him.

In one write-in campaign involving a seat in Congress, a precinct worker used a dog for this purpose. It was a cute dog, an English fox-terrier with two brown saddle spots on his side. He wore a placard on his body on which were printed the words "Precinct Chairman." He was bedecked in bright colored ribbons from which dangled yellow pencils bearing the name of the write-in candidate—correctly spelled. The voters stopped to look at the dog. They smiled and spoke to the little fellow admiringly. The worker merely said "don't forget" as he quietly gave each of them one of the yellow pencils. The dog's name was Tammy, but he did not hail from Tammany Hall. The election was in California. Tammy did a first class public relations job. He carried the precinct for the write-in candidate by a huge majority.

In this particular write-in election, a precinct organization had been set up in only eleven out of seven hundred eighty-four precincts. These eleven precincts were the only ones carried by the write-in candidate. Tammy's precinct was the banner precinct. Dogs know how to make friends.

If there is no Tammy available, there are other means of distracting the attention of the voter for those precious few seconds. In one write-in campaign a worker merely turned his eyes toward the heavens when the voters approached. There was nothing strange to be seen but the voter always stopped and looked upward. He found a pencil and a slip of paper in his hands as a reward for his sky gazing.

POSTSCRIPT

When the polls close on election night, the precinct worker snatches a sandwich, then waits for the fatal tally. A few hours later, when the neat little package in public relations is opened, he finds his reward.

If he has done his public relation's job as well as Tammy did his, the precinct has been carried.

Chapter XII

PUBLICITY AND PROPAGANDA

MANY of our most potent politicians never run for public office at all. They are the political press agents, the men and women who pull the strings, who set the stage, and by devices and procedures which we shall now discuss—mold and manipulate the mind of the electorate.

In politics, the press agent is expected to be a jack-of-all-trades. The average county committee or candidate is lucky to have as much as one competent publicity and propaganda expert. He is supposed to know something about:

> Creating gods and devils.
> Writing political platforms.
> Interpreting party programs.
> Getting up political "bibles."
> Preparing, making and disseminating news.

Writing advertising material.

Laying out advertising copy.

Making up special sheets.

Writing speeches and broadcasts.

Editing the party house organ.

Making reports to party officials.

Producing motion pictures.

Getting up meetings.

Organizing precinct workers.

Formulating campaign strategy.

If this isn't enough, it might be added that he is also supposed to know where the money bags are and how to tap them.

For this service the press agent may get a weekly stipend of fifty dollars. Very few reach the $100 a week class. And the "head" of the public relations department will be lucky if he collects all of his salary. If he fails to do so, he probably will be in the business of promoting bad public relations for someone in the next campaign.

GETTING MUCH FOR LITTLE

Politics is a low wage industry. This does not necessarily mean that the talent acquired is second or third rate, though often it is. For some inexplicable reason, perhaps sheer love of the game, men of outstanding ability in the field of political publicity and propaganda sometimes will sell their services at fantastically low figures.

In a small local campaign, it is often possible for a candidate to employ the part time services of a free lance newspaper reporter for as little as ten dollars a week. The services rendered for this small stipend may be of incalculable value. The free lance reporter usually makes it his business to be on intimate terms with the editors of the papers published in his district. Because he has protected them on many stories and done them other favors, these editors are glad to reciprocate and use his releases. A few small political advertisements thrown in for good measure as a token of appreciation always help to increase the number and size of news items accepted.

The hapless candidate who must manage his own publicity, sometimes is able to do very well even though entirely ignorant of the professional technique. If he has been in the habit of tipping off live news stories to the papers in his district, he may be very certain that his thoughtfulness will be appreciated. Not only is news of his own candidacy more likely to get better position, but reporters, not unmindful of the value and convenience of a live news source, may help in the preparation of releases. Many a politician has begun his upward climb by systematically communicating all sorts of news items, from society to crime, to his reporter friends.

Knowing a good printer also is an asset to the candidate with a slender purse. The printer will obligingly suggest when the copy is too crowded to be easily read, what type will be most attractive, and may take special pains in "make-up." Perhaps, if his search is diligent enough, the candidate may even find a professional press agent who without charge will help him prepare his material. Shrewd politicians have developed an uncanny knowledge of how to get little things done for nothing. Some even manage to get through their campaign without paying for anything!

In the small local campaign it is not vital, but it is handy to have a professional publicity agent on call; in other campaigns, such, for instance, as those involving a seat in Congress or the office of mayor or county supervisor in a populous community, a competent press agent becomes one of the "musts" of politics. Indeed, only the county committees in the smaller counties can afford, like the candidates, to conduct a campaign without such services.

There are times when publicity may be overdone. Interest in a campaign may mount so rapidly that organization is neglected or ignored. This often happens in a crusade. The workers are too busy cheering the cause to organize. They turn out in droves to the meetings, but they forget the precinct. This is one of the primary reasons that crusades so often fail. Propaganda is substituted for organization. The enthusiasm which is generated is not harnessed. Many now agree that Upton Sinclair's sensational Epic movement in 1934 might have succeeded if its adherents had spent less time applauding the speakers, and more time at work in the precinct trying to convince their less excited neighbors.

THE POLITICAL BLURB

Preparing, creating and disseminating news, getting up layouts, writing advertising copy, speeches and broadcasts are among the more routine chores of the political press agent. An extensive literature outlining successful methods used in this field is available to anyone who cares to examine it.

Party leaders and candidates need not seriously concern themselves with whether a news release should be double or single spaced, or limited to one page. The mechanical details of publicity and propaganda may safely be left to those who make these their business. A competent press agent also will understand the writer's technique, and his sense of news will tell him when he has gotten hold of something "hot." If he has a flare for wisecracking (which every political publicist should have), he will be on the alert for words to put in the candidate's mouth which will make the news columns. These do not necessarily need to refer to the campaign itself.

The really heavy tasks of the press agent in politics revolve around creating political gods and devils, writing and interpreting the platforms of the candidates and

parties, and getting up political "bibles." These assign-
ments all bear a close relation with each other and together strike the key for the campaign strategy.

There is nothing quite so compelling as a fact,
whether in politics or in the court room. And there do
happen to be voters who are moved by reason and truth.
To reach and convince that portion of the electorate
which insists upon being correctly informed, may determine the result of the election, for its influence on the
others is immense. The right five hundred voters will
convince the five hundred thousand.

HEAVENS AND HELLS

It is amazing how many elections are won in the
heavens above or lost in the seething pits of hell below.
In every campaign, big or little, it is wise to create a god
to love and a devil to hate. The political books are
filled with personal and impersonal gods and devils
playing their public relations roles in various manners.
In 1896, William Jennings Bryan was a political god
at whose feet millions of voters worshiped. Wall Street
was the Democratic devil who sought to seduce the people. Free Silver was the Koran from which millions took
their scripture. On the other hand, the Republicans had
a perfectly good Jehovah of their own. The Republican
god was gold; their devil was the specter of panic. The
full dinner pail was the holy book for the McKinley
legions.

Among the famous gods and devils of political history have been Nicholas Biddle and the Bank of the United States, Slavery, Green Backs, Prosperity, Woodrow Wilson, Private Initiative, the Non-Partisan League, the Big Stick, the New Deal, Huey Long, Populism, Peace, the Ohio Gang, the Ku Klux Klan, Rebellion and FDR.

In politics a bad devil is more potent than a good god. In the minds of the voters scourges are something to be done away with; the good things are taken for granted. "Turn the rascals out" remains as good a slogan today as it was a century ago.

A very astute political press agent has remarked that he never feels satisfied with what he has written unless the reader is moved to say that his candidate is "the greatest guy on earth" and that his candidate's opponent is a "dirty so-and-so."

This little emotional *coup d'état* is not engineered by direct praise or by name calling. On the contrary, the words must be so phrased that the voter himself will spontaneously express his likes and dislikes, if not vocally, at least inwardly.

ON MAKING THE ISSUE

Liquor, prostitution and gambling are favorite devils of reform groups in local campaigns. Usually the reformers make the fatal mistake of trying to cast out these devils by a frontal assault. It is not the little bookie the reform crowd is after, or the saloon keeper or the painted lady. It's the payoff to the police and to the law enforcement agencies which must be stopped if the decency and integrity of local democratic government is to be maintained.

Even members of the underworld have been known to agree with this line of propaganda. Many of them do not like payoffs, either. They would rather "reduce prices" and take their chances.

Vice should be incidental to the campaign, graft and bribery, the major issues.

Prohibition made little headway in America so long as its publicity bureaus talked about the evils of drink. It was only after its advocates convinced the voters that the liquor industry was controlling the politics of the nation that the 18th Amendment was adopted.

Few successful gods and devils are created out of the pure imagination of the publicist. Most of them are self made. Clever propaganda will quicken the affection of the voters for a great personality or intensify their passion for a new movement. However, the candidate must have the stuff out of which strong public figures are made, and the cause must have its base in sound human instinct and judgment. Also it must be remembered that though it is possible, by the adroit use of propaganda, to stimulate the natural tendency of people to hate, unless the object of their hate deserves much of the enmity, public sentiment is apt to change abruptly. The devil becomes a martyr; and martyrs do not lose elections.

The press agent who is a good politician (and many of them are), will not carry the devil business too far, particularly when the devil happens to be the opposition candidate. Nor will he over-play his hand by attempting to make a hero or a god out of an ordinary candidate. On the contrary, he will be entirely satisfied if he builds him from nothing to a position of sound mediocrity in the public eye. Regretfully, may we add, this is sufficient to win most campaigns.

Chapter XIII

POLITICAL "BIBLES"

POLITICAL "bibles" are a basic part of the publicity agent's kit. They are one of his most valuable tools. Unfortunately, they can be expensive tools and therefore are not always used. Many politicians and candidates do not even know what political bibles are.

The political bible is simply a detailed and indexed biography of the candidate. If a citizen has been in public life for a number of years, his bible may reach the size of a full sized book. One such bible, about the incumbent district attorney of a large metropolitan county, finally contained upwards of 300,000 words before he was defeated. In local campaigns for smaller offices, a bible may be only three or four pages long.

To the political press agent such bibles are practically indispensable, particularly when incumbents have been many years in the public service either as law makers or executives. In the case of the district attorney above mentioned, it required more than a year of one press agent's time to prepare that bible.

It is important both for the incumbent and his opponents to know what each has said and done while in public life. No item is so small or innocent looking that it can be overlooked. It may contain the name of some individual with whom an incumbent, for instance, was associated in a minor transaction many years previously. This information, long forgotten, pieced together with subsequent words and actions, may be the beginning of that tell-tale chain which finally connects him with a vice ring or some sort of organized official graft.

In the case of the district attorney that is what actually happened. The information, skillfully woven together, was used on the radio for months preceding the election by a civic leader who recognized the value of political bibles. The district attorney was defeated. The politicians, as usual, claimed the credit. Actually the election was won in the morgues of the newspapers, and in the library, where the old files were available. The campaign was won "between elections."

It is impossible to predict in a campaign just what issues may be raised. To be able to lift from a well indexed political bible *all* that the candidate has said or done relative to an issue which has suddenly become of great public interest, may be vital to the success of the campaign. If unexpected charges have been made, the press agent, by referring to the bible, is able to find the answer immediately. If queried for a statement, he can furnish it for the same issue of the paper in which the charge appears. He is not obliged to say "no comment until we have had an opportunity to examine the charge." He already has the facts. When the answer is delayed, the first impression is the one that usually sticks in the public mind.

In politics, it is well to remember that the people are inclined to believe the accuser because they regard all politics as "dirty," and, therefore, all politicians as guilty. For this reason it becomes doubly important for the accused to answer promptly and to take the offensive. He may either add a smear of his own, or decide that some constructive answer is better. But, no matter what the exact strategy decided upon, he must assume the role of the attacker instead of the attacked.

Besides a bible for his own candidate, the press agent also needs a bible containing all possible factual information about each of the principal opposing candidates. This information must be gathered a long time in advance, so that each item may be verified. Once a press agent is fortified with the facts he can bring his charges or countercharges with the assurance that they will not boomerang.

Political bibles are not campaign text books or flattering biographic sketches highly ornamented for the edification of the voters. They are a hard boiled summation of fact. Unfortunately, the candidate often is not candid with his own press agent. What the press agent wants to know is the worst that can be said against him. Instead the candidate is apt to tell the good and conceal the bad.

THE PARTY PLATFORM

In June, 1932, the Democratic national convention violated the rules of modern political tactics by adopting a short, concise platform which, among other things, promised that the federal budget would be balanced and that the expenses of government would be cut by at least twenty-five percent. The latter pledge was to be accomplished by the simple device of abolishing many of the agencies whose number had already begun to spiral during the Hoover administration. To have balanced the books eight months later, when Mr. Roosevelt became President, by sending tens of thousands of bureaucrats scurrying into the streets to sell apples, obviously would have intensified the panic and might have precipitated a revolution.

This period of kaleidoscopic changes, which we face in the years immediately ahead of us, seems to indicate that both Republicans and Democrats will engage in a great deal of double-talk. It probably will be a long time before a major political party again writes its platform in plain English.

Candidates dote on political platforms. Most of them

are willing to accept the party platform in toto whether they agree with it or not. But nearly every candidate wants to add something of his own. Examination of hundreds of different campaign leaflets and cards reveals that the "autobiographies" and "homemade" platforms of nearly all candidates for the smaller offices follow an almost identical pattern.

The candidate tells where he was born. If he is a native son his birthplace and local high school attendance is emphasized. Mention of the church he attends is very important if it happens to have a large membership in the district. Lodge, organization and club affiliations are supposed to make votes. These must be listed. The age and occupation of the candidate are of especial concern. The voters will be deeply concerned as to whether or not he is married, how many children he has, their sex, and whether he has always "been married to the same woman." If he is a member of the chamber of commerce, but "still carries a union card," so much the better.

Unabashed self praise always seems permissible in politics. A candidate must claim all the homely virtues. He must be honest, competent, intelligent, successful and above all a "fighter."

Mere enumeration of these "assets" is supposed to convince the voter that a candidate is qualified. But even this may not be enough. The candidate must have a platform. He spends a good many hours thinking about it. He will lose votes if he favors this; make enemies if he opposes that. So he solemnly confers with his friends and managers. Finally, the document is finished. The candidate believes in:

1. Honesty in government.
2. Strict economy.
3. Lower taxes.
4. A business administration.
5. Fair play for labor.
6. A square deal for business.
7. Courtesy in public office.
8. The Bill of Rights.
9. Upholding the Constitution.
10. Universal peace.

If pressed hard enough the candidate might be induced to add that he also believes in the Ten Commandments.

The slogans of the candidates who do their own composing are apt to be as trite and meaningless as their platforms. "They all call me Jim," or "Eternal Vigilance is the Price of Liberty" are good examples. Occasionally, the candidate tries to inject a bit of humor into his campaign slogan: "There is nothing 'Red' about Mike but his hair."

FEW CANDIDATES "LISTEN"

Ask the public relations department of any business to suggest its most difficult problem, and the reply usually is, "to sell the boss." The same is true in politics. To sell the candidate on the advantage of being different, or bold, or even half way intelligent in his public relations is the biggest hurdle of the press agent. The candidate who will listen is the press agent's delight. He may not always win. But he is sure to be a factor in the campaign. He will choose one or not more than two issues, and pitch his tent on a battlefield of his own selection.

Let us say, for example, that the candidate is running for the city council in a great metropolitan city. The sewerage system has been badly neglected. There has long been danger that the outfalls will burst. The ocean waters are (dangerously) polluted with solids and other filth oozing through holes in the submarine tube.

Politicians do not like to vote money for sewers. They prefer to spend the people's money on freeways, parks, airdromes and public buildings. These can be seen and admired by the taxpayer. It requires courage on the part of our candidate to urge that the people spend many millions of dollars to rehabilitate their sewerage system. Yet the job should be done. The facts warrant the expenditure.

For several years the health authorities and engineers have made plans and issued warnings. The reports and blueprints are gathering dust in the city's archives. The experts know what should be done but do not know how to dramatize the results of their investigations.

The work of the press agent now begins. The dust is removed from these old documents. The candidate begins to talk about the danger of disease, pestilence and death unless a new sewerage system is installed. Many miles of the city may be flooded with raw sewage if the outfall is not immediately repaired. The stench may drive thousands of families from their homes. The city will face a torrent of damage suits.

What the candidate says is supported by the statements of doctors and technical men whose standing in the community is not questioned. Informed opinion which has been latent or indifferent begins to make itself felt. People start talking about the candidate. He attracts a following. He does not need to boast that he is a "fighter"; he is already on the firing line. He is saying it by his actions. He charges that greedy contractors, more interested in selling cement than in building treatment plants, are responsible for the disgraceful and scandalous situation. The facts support him.

Typhus, cholera are the devils that must be cast out. The lives of the people must be spared.

The candidate himself is beginning to assume the

role of a hero. He has stolen the show from any opponent who is still talking about honesty in government, strict economy and a square deal for all.

If nothing serious goes wrong the candidate is elected. He may be a very mediocre person but by showing a little courage and being different he has impressed the electorate. And for that he can thank his press agent.

Political bibles on major problems, such as sewerage, transportation and others which may bob up at any time, are as important as bibles about political personalities.

Chapter XIV

THE ROSTRUM

THE style and manner of public speaking may have changed, but oratory is not yet a lost art. The power of the human voice to influence and persuade still excels. The written word is potent. When spoken in the rich Churchillian or Rooseveltian tones, it overwhelms.

Every politician cannot be an orator, but almost any politician can learn to speak well, with some training and (a great deal of) practice. He can be taught not to emphasize his *ands* and *buts* and the importance of nouns over adjectives.

There are a few men in public life who, like the late Colonel House, remain behind the curtain, yet exercise enormous power over political affairs. But the average politician, and particularly the aspirant for public office, who fails to attend meetings and make himself heard, has lost half the battle in his upward climb. There is nothing quite so compelling in a political campaign as a personal appearance and a good speech.

CHOOSING THE MEETING PLACE

Insofar as the spectacular "closing rally" in politics is concerned, there is little choice of the meeting place. Often there is only one auditorium available which will hold the crowd. But in the matter of the small local political meeting where, at the most, accommodations for only two or three hundred voters are required, there may be a number of places from which to choose. Selection of the right or wrong one among these may mean the difference between the success or failure of the meeting itself, and inevitably will affect the size of the audience when the next rally is advertised.

Indeed, much of the shyness on the part of the general public to attend the local political rally is because it has learned to expect poor accommodations and a frigid as well as a shabby performance.

In rural sections there is little choice of a meeting place. There is no other place to go except to the little red school house, lodge room, empty store or church. However, the rural voter will put up with almost anything because he is accustomed to the worst. He is more apt to attend the meeting because any public gathering is an event for him. Competition in public activities is not so intense as in the county seat town or the great urban area.

In the small town or city, the court room and city council chamber are ideal places in which to hold the political meeting. They are neither too large nor too small for the average turnout. The audience may smoke. There are even cuspidors. The people think of court houses and city halls in terms of politics. In this atmosphere they are not afraid to speak out. Furthermore the court room or city council chamber is usually conveniently located.

It is in the metropolitan area where the selection of the meeting place presents a really difficult problem in public relations.

Here, the school building is a good place to avoid. Politics and schools are divorced in the public mind. To the typical political audience schools mean restraint. The voter regretfully throws his cigarette away as he approaches the marble steps of the school building, or instinctively spits out his chewing gum. He feels that he must be on his good behavior. In the cold and forbidding hallway he hears no vigorous "Howdy, Bill!" With hushed voice he may speak to someone he knows. By the time he has quietly taken his seat he is mentally and psychologically prepared to listen to a formal lecture on the shifting of polar ice. Few political meetings held in big city school houses really get "warm."

The atmosphere of the large, spacious lodge room with its built-in seats around dismal walls and barren floor where the drill team practices, is scarcely more inviting. It is a bit hard on the speaker when there is no one seated in front of him and with perhaps only half the wall seats occupied, nor is it easy for the audience to follow the speaker who must pivot from side to side in order to give everybody a chance to see and hear him at least part of the time.

The unrented store room, usually dirty and often poorly lighted and ventilated, will not do at all. Churches, even were they more often available, are not good political meeting places, either. Political meetings are apt to develop a good deal of heat and passion and most people object to a "scene" in a house of worship.

In the big city there are always available many small lodges and other especially equipped halls which are fairly well ventilated and lighted, and which contain at least a few comfortable chairs together with light kitchen facilities. Here the audience may smoke, swear, interrupt, argue and raise general hell if it feels like it—which most political crowds inwardly do. Here the speaker has a chance to shake hands with everyone and get in that personal word which is often more important than the speech itself in establishing good public relations. People linger if they have had a good time at the meeting. And they will come again.

Incidentally, it is well to remember, sandwiches and coffee often compensate for a poor show.

SIZING UP THE AUDIENCE

Before a candidate prepares his speech, he should know something about the nature of the audience he is to address, and what may please or displease it.

If, for instance, he is to speak at a Nazarene meeting, he will avoid references to his fraternal affiliations. Nazarenes do not believe in fraternal societies because they require their members to take oaths. On the other hand, if he is to talk to a group of Presbyterians, it is well for him to say something about Roger Williams. He will be wise to refer to an authority the listener is accustomed to respect even though he may know little himself about that authority.

The rally of the 4th Ward Republican Club and a Kiwanis noon day luncheon are two different affairs. At each the speaker will be expected to show plenty of "pep." But the menus will differ. The party enthusiast is eager to consume raw political meat; the Kiwanian will devour a whole platter of subtle political implications, but the word politics is a nasty one, and is taboo.

At the general political rally where citizens other than strict party voters are present, the meat must be cooked a little longer. The speaker is there to convince as well as to impress. He must be more circumspect than at the hilarious party pow-wow.

The banquet hall has tripped many an otherwise fine speaker. Somehow a good Negro story goes with a plate of oysters and a dinner coat. If the speaker lacks the faculty of making people laugh after he has made his point, he might better decline the invitation to speak, or, if he does talk, he should stay in character and remain serious. There is nothing quite so flat as a Negro yarn spun in plain English, or quite so tragic as when it is told by a poor mimic.

Only the bravest of the brave will mount the rostrum at a county fair, barn dance or in the Yankee Stadium when a great sports event is on. The preparation of a speech for such occasions does not require the assistance of a press agent. When the speaker is introduced all he need do to establish perfect public relations with his audience is to rise, say "thank you," and sit down. The applause will be thunderous; the relief, both to the speaker and the crowd, even greater.

HARD WORK IS REQUIRED

Capable speakers often remark that they can talk but that they cannot write. They might more honestly have said that they can make a good speech but that they are too lazy to prepare it in advance. Had they possessed a little more energy, instead of delivering merely a good speech they might have made themselves famous as platform figures.

Like anything else, the preparation of a creditable talk involves hard work. There are many textbooks which will instruct the beginner in the methods of writing a speech. But there is nothing that will quite take the place of hard work and long practice. The safest procedure for the political candidate who is uncertain of himself is to consult his press agent, or employ a "ghost" writer. It is better to say something worth while at a political meeting, even if it does cost a little more, than to have a listener whisper to the voter in the next seat: "That speaker didn't have a thing to say!"

It is not essential that the candidate memorize the speech which has been prepared for him, though in some cases this improves the delivery. But it is advisable that the sequence be "photographed" on the speaker's mind, and that the climaxes be committed to memory. Many a speech which contains excellent material is ruined because the speaker failed to arrange his thoughts in an orderly manner, or neglected to drive them home by strong, vivid phrases injected in the right place at the right moment. It is always dangerous for a speaker to rely entirely on inspiration. It may fail him at precisely the wrong moment.

Because relatively few voters attend local political meetings, it is of great importance to the speaker that his words be picked up and quoted by the press. Speeches should be prepared with this thought in mind. The speaker who has shown some originality is almost sure to be among the ones quoted. The names of the others will be listed among those who "also spoke."

Often, no newspaper reporter is present at the small

political rally. In that event the candidate who has prepared his speech and who has left a copy of it at the local newspaper office, may get his name in the headlines while the other speakers are ignored. If the subject is a timely one and the speech contains good reader material, it may get a much bigger play than the speaker would dared to have prayed for.

THE CANDIDATE'S PLACE ON PROGRAM

During the course of a campaign, the candidate usually makes a great many platform appearances. At some meetings he is the principal, perhaps the only speaker; at others, one among several. Obviously, he cannot take the time to prepare a new speech for every meeting, or one that will fit the time allowance on each program. A comparatively easy method of overcoming this obstacle is to prepare one main speech. This should be so arranged that it can be broken down and divided into a number of speeches, each, with slight variation, complete in itself. Thus a forty-five minute speech can be so written that it is easily divisible into one thirty and one fifteen minute, or into two fifteen and three five minute, talks, depending upon the subjects that must be covered. While this procedure may require additional effort in the first instance, it will save a great deal of time as the campaign progresses.

Except when he has arranged his own meeting or is

the only person on the program, the candidate is faced with one of those seemingly unimportant public relations chores which may mean so much. He must spar for position on the program. Unless actually in a hurry to get away, it is not advisable for him to speak first, unless the audience is seated and quiet. Then it may be an advantage, particularly if the speaker makes a good impression. The first impression always counts so heavily. To be the last speaker is not desirable, either, unless the program is a short one.

It too often happens that the principal speaker is the very one reserved for the last. He is supposed to "climax" the meeting. The lesser lights will be able to have their say if they come on ahead of the more distinguished guest. It is presumed that the audience will remain until the end.

Should you be the candidate who is cast in the main speaker's role, insist that you be placed somewhere else than last on the program. The main speaker should always insist on having the best, not the worst place on the program.

Where vaudeville and other stunts are included on the program, the speaker will be wise if he insists that he speak before the entertainment. On such convivial and hilarious occasions, the crowd will wait until midnight to see the scantily clad dancer. But when she has twitched her last muscle, there is apt to be a stampede for the exits. In such circumstances the speaker begins his remarks in the presence of the faithful few who felt it was their duty to remain. And they will all be looking at their watches!

PLATFORM TECHNIQUE

Before a candidate begins to worry about when he should wave his arms, ruffle his hair and twist his features, he should think about wearing a clean shirt, a good looking tie and a dignified suit of clothes.

A great many people go to see and not to hear a public speaker. Even though the speech be pretty bad, it will help if the candidate looks like a statesman.

The Socialists learned this lesson many years ago in Wisconsin. They discovered that a working man, dressed in overalls and greasy from work, did not make a hit even with his own crowd. The Socialist vote took a sudden spurt when their candidates began to appear well groomed. A white shirt and polished shoes do a lot in promoting good public relations. Ordinarily, an audience does not feel flattered when it is addressed by someone who looks more like a tramp than a candidate for public office. (The late Heywood Broun could fascinate his hearers despite his baggy pants and ruffled collar, but the Heywood Brouns are exceptions.)

Discovering the secret of making a creditable platform appearance is in part a matter of learning what not to do.

Don't lean on a chair. Don't stand behind a table. The

audience came to see you, not the furniture. Don't keep looking at your watch. If you are doing all right, your listeners are not interested in what time it is. Don't pause for a drink of water. It will only increase your thirst a few minutes later and remind the audience that it has been a long time between drinks. Don't keep mopping your face and blowing your nose with a handkerchief. The people know how hot it is, and if you have a cold you have no business being where you are. Don't look at the ceiling.

Don't try to imitate a ham actor by gesticulating wildly or by indulging in facial contortions. There is a theater just around the corner where the audience can see the real thing. Don't strike Shakespearean poses. People know you are not Hamlet.

A college course in public speaking is not required to teach the speaker how to act on the political rostrum. He will give his best performance when he does not think at all about his hands, feet, eyes, nose and hair. But a few lessons on how to use his voice, on the emphasis of words and what is meant by a change of pace and timing, may be very helpful.

One other don't: if you intend to leave personalities out of your speech, don't begin by telling your audience that you are not going to "knock" your opponent or "throw any mud." Your listeners will be disappointed. They came for the "fireworks" and here you are announcing in advance that you have no Roman candles, sky rockets or giant crackers to set off. If you have no charges to make, don't admit it. Just go ahead with your speech. The audience itself, in due course, will discover that you have a "constructive message."

There are a few simple rules governing the best things to do when you occupy the political rostrum.

Begin the speech with a strong statement, something that will jolt the audience. This will bring immediate attention even if people are still coming in. If the hour is late, an unusual or sensational opening remark may be enough to hold the voters in their seats. Always keep the audience in suspense as long as possible. It is more apt to stick around.

During the speech, if someone starts to leave and people turn to stare, stop talking. The chances are that you will immediately recapture the attention of the listeners, who realize they are not being polite.

Most speakers crave applause, but at the right time. If some enthusiastic friend in the audience starts applauding before you get your point over, see him outside after the meeting and warn him that he is hurting the cause. Too much applause, particularly at the wrong time, can ruin a good speech. The audience simply cannot sustain its thought long enough to follow the speaker when the speech is interrupted. Frequent applause also is convincing evidence that the speaker's appeal is almost entirely emotional. People do not interrupt with applause when they are trying to think.

The speaker should wind up his talk on a strong, positive, emotional note. Don't apologize because you have "talked too long." If you have, the audience already is painfully aware of it. But a powerful climax may cause it to forget an exceeded time limit.

Finally, it is especially important that the speaker does not work himself into such a frenzy that he forgets what his final words are to be. That is exactly what happened to the brilliant Republican district attorney at the end of a big Landon-for-President rally in 1936.

"In the name of liberty, democracy and of the vast majority of the American people, I ask you to vote for that great and eminent American statesman . . . that great and eminent . . . that great . . ."

The speaker could not think of his candidate's name.

"Franklin Delano Roosevelt!" shouted a political rogue in the gallery.

HANDLING HECKLERS AND MOBS

Often a speaker is interrogated by someone in the audience before he has concluded. It is usually enough if he suggests politely that he would prefer to answer questions when he has finished his remarks. If this does not satisfy the audience, he might just as well begin the battle of wits with the hecklers at once. If he comes out on top, as any speaker should who has the advantage of the platform, he may make more votes than if he had continued his speech without interruption.

The odds are heavy that the heckling will not continue in good spirits. There is nearly always someone in the crowd who has become angry at the speaker, or nurses a political grudge against him. He is there to embarrass. His question is apt to be couched in insolent words. It is designed more to belittle the candidate than to provide the audience with enlightenment.

All that the speaker need do is to remark that he will be pleased to answer all questions except those which are abusive and plainly vicious in intent.

"Yes, he will be happy to reply to the gentleman, if he will behave like a *gentleman!*"

The effect is instantaneous. Whatever it may have been before, sentiment now definitely shifts to the side of the speaker. It was unfair, anyway, to interrupt the speaker! The candidate is being persecuted! That fresh guy oughta be thrown out! The crowd is stirred. It seeks reprisals against the interloper.

The candidate has kept his head. He has smiled and been good natured. He has answered the real questions. Now he has complete command of the situation. His relations with his audience actually have been improved. He is free to proceed.

Occasionally, the technique fails to work. The audience is there to "get the speaker." It was mad before it came. Heckling will not satisfy its lust to punish, because of some fancied wrong the candidate has done the people or is about to attempt. The audience resorts to a real demonstration. It shouts, stamps its feet, shakes its fists, begins to march around the hall.

It means business.

The speaker smiles. He continues to smile just as if the audience were demonstrating for instead of against him. He shows no trace of fear. There is no chip on his shoulder, either. He is not inviting more trouble than he already has.

He knows that basically a mob is a craven, cowardly creature. He also knows that in every political mob there will be some persons ready to defend him. If he attempts to leave by the rear exit he may be sure that he will be pursued. The crowd will gain courage. The culprit must be guilty or he would not attempt to flee.

The speaker chooses, instead, to leave the same way he arrived, by the front entrance. Without showing the slightest concern he walks up the aisle. He observes three or four members of the audience following him closely. Perhaps someone is just ahead of him. He is reassured. He knows he has friends and that they are not afraid to use their fists. He keeps smiling. And now he is also talking like a chatter box!

"Sure wish I had this crowd with me. . . . Never saw so much spirit. . . . Sorry you didn't like the speech. . . . Will try to do better next time. . . . I'm not such a bad guy when you get to know me. . . . There's a lot o' you and mighty few o' me. . . . Glad the Yanks won today. . . . Fine evening. . . . !!!!"

The crowd is caught completely by surprise. It had expected its intended victim to shake with fear, plead for mercy. Before it can collect itself, the speaker is outside.

Then he runs for his car!

His public relations have been nothing to brag about, but he has saved his hide.

BEWARE THE DEBATE

Challenges to debate are no longer commonplace in American politics. Because the element of personal conflict is present, debates will draw larger crowds than the ordinary political meeting the same as a football game will attract more people than afternoon practice by one of the teams.

Even so, a good speaker will hesitate before he accepts an invitation to debate. The public relations of the participants can go up or down in a hurry at such events. Unless he is very certain he can win, it is best for the candidate to avoid the challenge.

The inexperienced speaker has no business at all in the debate arena. Here there will be no press agent, campaign manager or friend to whisper advice in his ear. He will be strictly on his own. The public relations results are apt to be catastrophic.

GO WHERE THE VOTERS ARE

Perhaps it is because politics has become a wholesale rather than a retail business that the purely political rostrum is so much on the decline as an effective instrument for reaching the voters in all but the smallest political units. Or, it may be that oratory as an art is gradually disappearing.

Instead of arranging his own meetings, the candidate is finding it increasingly necessary to go where the crowds are. He asks for five minutes at the labor union or lodge meeting. He pulls wires to get before the Parent-Teachers Association and other organizations and groups, if only to take a bow. He prefers to make a non-political speech at a meeting of the Chamber of Commerce than a political speech to empty chairs. These are ominous portents in the modern democratic world.

Several years ago a youthful politician was booked for a number of speeches in a campaign in Texas. Only a few voters came to hear him, though he spoke especially well. Finally, one Saturday afternoon he mounted the bandstand in the public square of a small county seat town and in a few moments several hundred farmers and town folk had gathered to hear what this unannounced speaker had to say.

Unfortunately, our young man had not calculated the number and variety of counter attractions in that small Texas town on a hot Saturday afternoon. He was scarcely well under way with his speech before he heard shouts and a great commotion across the street.

There, to his astonishment, was a man holding an ugly creature aloft in outstretched hands.

"Right this way," he was shouting. "Right this way! I'm gonna put ma finga in the rep-*tile's* mouth! I'm gonna put ma finga in the *rep-tile's* mouth!"

The ambitious young orator, with no crowd of his own, spent the remainder of the afternoon listening to the pitchman who was selling some kind of a contraption for taking internal baths and guaranteed to cure everything from gout to heart disease.

That evening our despondent youth had a bright idea. He decided to go where the crowds were and to make his speeches there. He agreed to give the snake-charmer two dollars for twenty minutes' time at each of his "shows." Two, three, sometimes four times a day after that the young man spoke to the only real crowds he had seen. The candidate he was sponsoring for governor won.

Chapter XV

INFORMATION PLEASE

QUIZZING the political candidate is one of the favorite pastimes of citizens' groups and committees.

Aspirants for the higher offices often escape the barrage of questionnaires, "candidates' meetings" and privately conducted inquisitions by special committees which characterize election periods, but the ordinary candidate is constantly harassed by all sorts of organizations whose mania for "information" about the local candidate and his views is an accepted and praiseworthy democratic habit.

Imagine yourself, for instance, a candidate for the city council in a good sized American municipality. It is your first attempt to gain public office. You realize your new stature in the community by the almost immediate increase in your incoming mail. A few friends congratulate you. Some inform you you're a fool for venturing into political life.

Among the more bulky letters, sure to reach you, are the questionnaires. You will be lucky if you receive no more than a dozen of these formidable looking, ominous sounding brain twisters. You are more likely to find twice that number in your mail, each accompanied by a letter warning that the enclosure should be answered and returned promptly. Often a deadline is fixed. The committee which passes on the answers is about to meet! Your reply must be in on time if you expect your candidacy to receive consideration! "If we do not receive the material directly from you, we shall be forced to get it elsewhere, and so indicate in our handbook!"

THE BARRAGE OF QUESTIONS

Across the top of the letterhead may be a highly colored streamer suggesting the importance of the group, and perhaps indicating its primary aim. The names of its more important sponsors appear on the margins. The name of the organization sounds impressive. Often it is an "institute" of some sort. The letter itself is carefully phrased.

To you whose hat is in the ring for the first time it probably will seem that your entire political career is written in the pages of these questionnaires. You look at some of the questions:

"What plan do you propose for dealing with (a) the liquor problem, (b) commercialized gambling, (c) organized vice?"

Not such a tough one, you muse, yet the question has its embarrassing aspects.

"Do you think it possible for city government to establish a labor mediation board or some such device for minimizing strife between labor and industry?"

"What do you think of the borough system of government?"

"What are your ideas on the abolition of the present Permanent Improvement Fund, or its being earmarked for specific permanent improvements?"

Frankly, you are stumped!

You observe that the questionnaires total more than 150 questions.

Now your eyes focus on a question that requires a categorical "yes" or "no" answer. The committee is not going to let you escape on this one. No explanation; no equivocation. You are in the trap. You happen to know a good deal about this subject. And because of this you know that its intelligent treatment is impossible without discussing the hundred and one "ifs" which are vital in reaching the right answer. These "ifs" could fill a book. Right now you have no ambition to become an author.

The experienced politician doesn't even blink when he nonchalantly examines "another of these damned questionnaires." Often he does not look farther than the name on the letterhead. He already knows which organizations are effective as well as which, though sincere in their motives, think they are effective, but actually have no real influence. The sophisticated politician always keeps a waste basket handy. His time is too valuable in the final stages of a campaign to attempt to establish friendly public relations with small, well-intentioned groups which are incapable of putting a sizable number of votes in the ballot box.

It is extremely important that the candidate know the background of such organizations, their dominating ideology, and something about their leaders before he attempts to reply to the questionnaire. Perhaps it will be just as well not to answer at all. So far as answering questionnaires is concerned, the public relations job of the candidate finally resolves itself into establishing friendly contact with, and winning the support of, the relatively few important groups which he is sure will give his candidacy conscientious consideration.

Satisfactorily answering the questionnaires of such groups is not as difficult a mental and psychological feat as one might imagine.

Often the way a particular question is asked, reveals the answer which the committee would like to have. If the candidate is at all uncertain about how he should reply in order to please the leaders of the group, there are ways of finding out. Probably the experienced candidate already has his "pipeline" laid. He knows as much, or more, about the inner workings and feelings of the committee which judges the questionnaire as the members themselves know. Through confidential sources he is already familiar with what was said by each of the committeemen when the questionnaire was prepared. In short, he knows why the several questions were included.

However, too pat an answer may arouse the suspicion of an unbiased, enlightened committee and result in an unfavorable reaction. Therefore, in some cases, it probably is best that the candidate state his position boldly, and as intelligently as possible. If he is not sure of the answer to a question, it may profit him frankly to confess his ignorance. That rare civic creature, the genuinely open minded committee, is not expecting complete acquiescence with its own views. It is not looking for "yes" men. It actually welcomes divergence of opinion. It is more impressed by the spirit of the answers of the candidate than by his opinions on a particular subject. Such a committee is looking for that fearless, independent expression which is so uncommon among those seeking political preferment.

On a whole the political questionnaire is an overrated method of correctly appraising the qualifications or ascertaining the real attitude of a candidate. Both the quizzers and the quizzed lack complete sincerity.

To save face and give the appearance of fairness the committee mails its questionnaire to *all* of the candidates, knowing quite well that the answers of most of these candidates, no matter how satisfactory, will receive no consideration at its hands. Political groups have no appetite for candidates whose chances of election are nil. Nor are such groups in the business of promoting the election of those who may win, but who may oppose their own pet ideas and plans. To burden a member of a different political school with a questionnaire, well knowing that on that account his candidacy will not be favorably considered, is merely another form of political hypocrisy and illusion.

PUBLIC AND PRIVATE INQUESTS

The quizzers slyly set the questionnaire trap hoping to catch one or more candidates in commitments which will bind their future policy and conduct. Aware that the trap is being laid, the smart candidate just as cunningly plans to eat the cheese without releasing the spring. The candidate knows that his public relations job is to provide all the information he can without promising more than his conscience and convictions will permit, nor more than he can reasonably perform.

Happily, comparatively few organizations make it a practice of seeking information by sending out questionnaires. The community improvement association, the district political club, the pension group, labor union or other local organization usually prefer to send for the candidates themselves. Sometimes the candidates are invited to a public meeting for a one-round battle royal; again they may be summoned to appear singly before a solemn looking committee whose members, pencil and pad in hand, glare at their victims with the ferocity of a lion ready for the kill.

Most of the so-called "candidates' meetings" where each hopeful is limited to a two or three minute speech, followed later by a short question period, remind one more of the parade of a bevy of pretty girls at a beauty contest than they do of a political acrobatic show in which the participants are supposed to exhibit their mental powers rather than their bodily graces.

The small, private committee hearing where the candidate takes his individual political turn is a more solemn political gag. Here, no bow is required, and a smile or laugh is as out of order as a highball at a church vesper. There is a tense attitude as the candidate enters the room and is motioned to a chair. The neophyte knows now what it means to be on the political "hot seat." Questions are shot at him from every angle, some of them foolish, others tinged with irony, and still others calculated to trap or embarrass him. Now and then it is apparent that a question has been inspired by someone who does not exactly like him. In from five to fifteen long and dreadful minutes the inquisition is over. The candidate is told to leave. Another victim is ushered in.

The experienced candidate is no more impressed with this type of a quiz program than he is with the questionnaire. He knows the relative strength of the several groups, and he knows which are phony. Wisely, the political veteran has laid his pipelines into each of these groups weeks, perhaps months, before he is summoned to appear before them officially. He has carefully chosen his friends, perhaps given private assurances of his position to the leaders. He has been tipped off on how to parry each embarrassing question. He has set his public relations straight with those who count most before either the public or private inquest takes place. He knows the correct name of the song before it is played. He attends the meeting merely because it is "the thing to do." To show himself will not change the verdict.

It is when revolt within a group threatens, or the decision is a genuinely open one, that even the political general has his uneasy moments. Indeed, it is never quite safe for any candidate to attend any meeting or hearing without being prepared for that emergency or unexpected turn which are so common where personalities and public policies are involved. There is always the danger that someone else will steal the show.

Because the candidate is limited to a three minute talk does not mean that he can't say something worth while. There is no need of wasting words on pleasantries. Three minutes' time is ample to get across a stirring appeal. It took Lincoln only two minutes to deliver his Gettysburg Address. The shorter the time allowance, the greater the effort the candidate should put forth in his preparation. Almost anyone can say something if he has an hour in which to say it; most candidates say nothing when they are confronted by the purely psychological barrier of "not enough time."

The shrewd candidate is always looking for the quisling in the quiz pile. The manner in which he pursues his public relations with groups which thrive on questionnaires, candidates' meetings and private inquisitions will depend upon the sincerity and integrity of their leaders and the political strength of such groups. If the cards are stacked against him, he will expend his efforts in other directions. If it's a game of manipulation, the candidate will bring out his own bag of tricks. If the group and its leaders are powerful, and objective in their attitude, and if they are sincerely concerned with the general public interest, the wise candidate will be as frank, bold and generous with his opinions and knowledge as his intelligence and personality permit.

Chapter XVI

STRATEGY

A FEW drops of rain cost Napoleon the Battle of Waterloo. The over-confident conqueror unnecessarily delayed his attack just long enough to enable General Bluecher's army to re-inforce Wellington at the critical moment.

In politics, as in war, timing is the greatest single factor in successful strategy. Elections are not won the day before the polls open or the day after the polls close. Every shrewd candidate tries to plan his campaign so that his maximum strength will be felt on election day. Old timers still reminisce about the three Bryan campaigns when the Peerless One from Nebraska always won the Presidency in September and lost it in November.

In the political campaign, something more than good public relations is required. The best public relations must be arrived at during the few fleeting hours the polls are open.

In both the 1936 and 1940 Presidential campaigns, Mr. Roosevelt did an outstanding job in political timing. During the summer and early fall of these years he said nothing, notwithstanding the fact that Mr. Landon in 1936, and Mr. Willkie four years later, had ceaselessly bombarded his administration for months, and that much of the nation's press had continuously and severely criticized him for a long time before that. Anyone who visited one of the numerous Democratic headquarters during this period of around-the-clock Republican attacks, will recall the growing tension among the party leaders at the President's delay in firing his first shot. By late September it began to look as if Mr. Roosevelt planned to let the election go by default. Many of the small fry politicos were in a panic.

But the President had guessed right. The people had heard all that they wanted, and more, from Mr. Roosevelt's traducers. When he finally broke his silence, he spoke to a record breaking audience. Everyone wanted to hear what the President of the United States had to say. The enemy had already worn itself out. Its guards were down. A haymaker provided the knockout.

Wendell Willkie's campaign collapse in the spring of 1944, was, in the opinion of many analysts, due to the fact that he talked too long and too much too early in the campaign.

TIMING IN LOCAL CAMPAIGNS

It is in campaigns for the smaller offices that proper timing becomes extremely difficult. There are seldom reliable polls to indicate the drift of popular opinion. Usually the candidate must sense how rapidly sentiment is crystallizing for or against him. He is seldom entirely certain just when to give his workers the go sign for the big drive, or exactly when he should signal "bombs away" and release his propaganda block busters.

Generally speaking, most candidates begin their active campaigning too early. During the time they should be planning and preparing, they are already conducting an enthusiastic canvass. An incumbent, however, is less apt to make this mistake than a challenger, because the former usually has a better line on public sentiment, as well as because his organization is more or less permanent. He knows that he has the facilities for quick, decisive movement.

Public issues also have a great deal to do with timing. It may be a year when everyone is talking politics because there are highly controversial questions to be settled. A crusade may be on. In that event, sentiment will crystallize rapidly. The candidate must make his views known and his influence felt before his opponent gets a firm grip on the ball. Or, it may be a quiet election year. Then the voter takes little interest in politics. Under such circumstances, and assuming that he is prepared for the last minute blitz, the candidate may wisely reserve his ammunition until a few days before the voting. When he risks everything on a single throw of the dice, he must be sure that the dice are properly loaded and that the right numbers will show.

CHARGES AND COUNTER CHARGES

If a candidate has a serious charge to make against an opponent, he should not wait until the last moment to make it. Good sportsmanship is almost a religion with the average American. Even if he is inclined to believe the charges he resents an eleventh hour smear which gives the accused no time to answer. Only if it involves a point which could not have been earlier revealed because it was not known to the accuser will it be accepted by the voters as made in good faith, and be considered on its merits.

Whenever possible, it is always good strategy for a candidate to break down an opponent a step at a time. If he has sensational information capable of being developed into a first class political drama, he should not begin with the climax. Like the clever playwright, he should hold his audience in suspense by revealing small bits of villainy first and reserving the real act of perfidy for the last. By that time the voters are ready to boil the villain in oil.

On the other hand, the best defense for the candidate

under attack, is to anticipate the climax and answer the charges in advance. The accused may have no real answer for the charges. But he can divert public attention from the scandal and focus it on the motives of the accuser. In politics as in war, the best defense is an offense.

It is astonishing how many candidates for political office try to conceal the weak spots in their records, both private and public. Yet all of them know that the opposition, in all probability, will discover the bad things and use them in the campaign. The sooner a candidate acknowledges his mistakes, the better off he will be. He can then take the offensive and keep it.

Often a candidate unexpectedly is subjected to an especially vicious and untruthful attack made by someone other than his opponent. If the accuser is a reputable citizen, it is best in such cases to call on him in person and prove to him that his charges were based on unreliable or inaccurate information. An apology is sure to follow. On the other hand, if the attack is made by someone whose reputation is bad and who is notoriously known as a "smear artist," the incident may wisely be ignored. The influence of such persons is never great. It is often a good omen if a candidate finds that they are against him.

Again, an accusation made in bad faith may be a political decoy designed to divert public attention from the real campaign issues. To call on the accuser and attempt to explain is a waste of time. Indeed, such a call may inspire a fresh and more ruthless assault. It will be interpreted as weakness.

It would be much better if the accused merely gave out a brief statement denying the charges, exposing their source, and emphasizing that he is determined to continue to discuss the really important issues of the campaign.

ATTITUDE TOWARD OPPONENTS

Primary campaigns in which a number of candidates are competing, present another perplexing problem in election strategy. Here each candidate has a two-fold public relations job to do. He must win the good will of the voter, but he must also keep the good will of some or all of his opponents. If he is nominated he will want, and probably need, the support of the candidates he defeated. This will be particularly true where a run-off is provided and the finals are between the two highest, with the names of the other candidates dropped.

Where possible, it is obviously to the advantage of the candidate if he does not attack any of his opponents personally. Opponents with no chance to win should never be attacked. It is much better to have a friendly word for them. This strategy may pay big dividends when the primary is over.

ONE BATTLE IS ENOUGH

Again and again a candidate makes the fatal mistake of taking on too many battles. Sometimes he is not even satisfied to confine his remarks to his opponents. His strategy seems to be to make enemies, not friends. He challenges all comers, whether they are running against him or for some other office. He itches for a fight just to be fighting. His behavior is comparable to that of a merchant who would deliberately seek more competitors because he believes in competition.

Many a candidate rides into office on someone else's coattails, Mr. Roosevelt's, for instance. This may be the only sound strategy for the candidate who lacks personality and is none too popular.

Unfortunately, there is no trustworthy rule to follow in reaching decisions affecting these various and complex situations. But one thing is certain: a candidate must make up his mind, after studying the political currents, as to the particular strategy he will follow. He cannot, to paraphrase Stephen Leacock, mount his political steed and ride off in all directions at one time.

OTHER STRATAGEMS

Two of the most obscure yet important factors in political strategy are when and where the candidate should begin his speaking campaign, and how he is to proceed when his budget precludes an active, organized campaign throughout his district.

If he has made up his mind a long time in advance to toss his hat in the ring, the answer insofar as it concerns the first of these problems is plain; he should manage some way to appear before as many organizations and groups in his district as possible. His speeches should not be strictly political, yet so presented that he establishes himself as a well informed citizen, particularly as to those problems in which his audiences are vitally interested. If the candidate has made a favorable impression, and if he does a little clever maneuvering, there will be a demand for him to make the race. If he does not appear over-anxious to be a candidate, he will develop still more strength. Finally, he may expect to be "drafted."

If he has failed to do his political plowing early, an entirely different problem confronts the candidate. Then it is not so much when, but where he will deliver his keynote speech. It should be a good one. Most candidates conclude that they should open their campaign where they have the fewest friends. They want to build up sentiment for themselves. They think they must invade their opponent's strongholds first.

Exactly the opposite is the proper strategy. A merchant does not begin by spending large sums of money advertising his wares where he has few customers. He introduces his merchandise where he is already favorably known. He relies on satisfied customers to extend his reputation to other places. The wise head makes his first speech where he believes there will be the most warmth and enthusiasm. This is usually in his own neighborhood or community. He will have a bigger crowd. His friends will be encouraged. If he makes mistakes, his neighbors will overlook them. He will learn how to improve his speech. The warmth and enthusiasm of his reception will spread. The "cold spots" will not be quite so cold.

There are times, however, when it is advisable for a candidate to make his first talk outside of his own district. He experiments. He discovers what pleases and what displeases; where to add and where to subtract; what points go over and which of his statements fall flat. Thus he perfects his performance, and learns how to keynote when the proper time comes.

When to set the wheels of his organization in motion, and where to concentrate, also are extremely important factors in political strategy. The candidate with a bagful of money, and whose campaign is moving, can safely delay the precinct work until the latter stages of the campaign. Political workers, like athletes, perform best when they are on edge. It is wiser to start them on their rounds a little late than too early.

It is when a candidate cannot afford to place a complete organization in the field that he must start much sooner. He is not going to be able to reach every voter in the final stretch because there are not enough workers to do the job thoroughly in the limited time that is available. In such circumstances, it is often advisable for the candidate not even to attempt to reach every voter in his district. On the contrary, he may find it advantageous to concentrate all of his efforts in a relatively small area. If he can procure an overwhelming majority in a contiguous block of fifty out of two hundred precincts he may win because his opponents have split the vote elsewhere. Or, perhaps, he should checkerboard the district, concentrating in one precinct, skipping three. The heat generated in the precincts which have been intensively canvassed, may radiate and warm up those precincts which the candidate has been obliged to neglect.

This strategy often succeeds. In Illinois it is nearly always a question of whether the Democratic majority in Chicago can overcome the Republican majority down state. The Cook county candidate is almost sure to win if his opponents divide the vote outside of the city of Chicago.

The merchant who gets all the business in his own neighborhood and some of his business elsewhere, is almost certain to enjoy a more profitable season than his competitors who divide the patronage of the entire community.

We have already mentioned tides, crusades and gum-shoe campaigns. When these occur the problem of timing is simple. In the case of tides and crusades, get on the band wagon early and stay there. In the gum-shoe campaign, start early and never stop!

Chapter XVII

SEX AND SALESMANSHIP ON
THE POLITICAL FRONT

AMERICAN women have arrived in politics in force. They do most of the precinct work, act as bureau heads and sometimes serve as managers in political headquarters. They are performing innumerable political chores once exclusively reserved for the male politician. Through their study clubs and other groups, women threaten to monopolize the field of fact finding, public research, of assemblying and correlating reliable information, particularly in local political campaigns.

Women have time to attend lectures, men do not. The feminine sex has taken over nearly all of the strictly social functions of politics. Women already have occupied some of the inner trenches of man's last political defense line. They have been elected to Congress, to the United States Senate, and have governed States.

To win the "women's vote" is supposed to guarantee

victory at the polls. Nearly every candidate, at least for major office, has one speech, one piece of campaign literature for women only. He imagines there is one set of political virtues which appeal to women as distinct from men. Thus we have double-track political campaigns in which groups of organized women and groups of perspiring candidates, each striving to understand the other, pass each other in the dark without sign of recognition.

REACTIONS SIMILAR

Actually, most public opinion polls show that men and women react almost alike to candidates and political issues, even in those instances where personal and public morality are paramount in the public mind. A difference of ten percent in the attitude of men as distinguished from that of women is rare. Even five percent is unusual. In most cases the polls show that the difference in viewpoint is negligible.

An examination of numerous registration lists in the great polyglot city of Los Angeles shows that about eighty-eight percent of all married couples registered in the same political party either as Republicans, Democrats or under one of the minor party designations. Undoubtedly the percentage would be much higher were such lists examined in overwhelmingly predominant Republican or Democratic sections of the nation, such as in the Solid South, or in Maine and Vermont.

Members of the same immediate family usually have a strong political affinity. In the relatively few cases where there is an estrangement, the votes of husband and wife simply cancel themselves out.

It is well for a candidate to bear in mind that the political program which appeals most to thoughtful men nearly always appeals also to thoughtful women; that women voters resent being patronized and humored, and that in some respects they are more sensitive than men about political sops thrown to them. Women are more apt to vote for the candidate who is frankly masculine in his political attitude toward women than for the candidate whose appeal seeks to create sex vanity or sex distinctions. That women are unmoved by special appeals to them is further evidenced by their repeated refusal, as women, to support women candidates for public office.

In short, the so-called "women's vote" in politics is a myth. No candidate should deceive himself into thinking otherwise because here and there some feminine leader is politically sex conscious. Such women often are vociferous and manage to get their names in the papers. They do not influence many women.

WOMEN AS WORKERS

Selecting women for the various official tasks of a political campaign presents an entirely different problem.

Women, for instance, seldom make popular managers of campaign headquarters. Other women become extremely jealous of them; men workers sullenly resent the choice. Whether or not the particular woman selected is competent, seems to make little difference. Psychologically, things do not click.

The employees' relations in private industry often suffer in like manner when a woman is given a "man's job." But the employees must carry on just the same. In politics, however, the workers have nothing to lose by shirking. Most of them are not paid. The campaign lasts only a few weeks. Before adjustment is possible, the election is over. Now and then a woman is found who can command the respect of the men and women workers alike. Such a personage is as priceless in politics as the Sultan's jewels.

Generally speaking, women serve best in the precinct, in drives for small campaign contributions, as propagandists in their own districts, and as leaders of study clubs. Here we find large sectors of the political battle-front which have been almost entirely evacuated by men; strategic passes through which political armies must move in order to invade enemy territory successfully.

Men have been glad to delegate the hard work of the precinct canvass to women; to let them make the search for the pennies, nickels and dimes; to give them the job of properly distributing campaign literature to the homes; to allow women to monopolize the small study groups where political thinking is taken seriously.

As women learn to do these chores efficiently they will climb to political leadership. Because they will come to know and understand the voter better than men, they are sure ultimately to be given, or to usurp, many of the larger, though no more important, public relations jobs in politics.

OPTIMISTS AND EGOTISTS

It is never wise for a politician to suggest that he is "gaining" because it implies that he is behind. It is better to say that he is "increasing his lead." There is an old adage that "any kind of publicity is better than no publicity." This is nonsense. To comment that a candidate has no chance is far more hurtful than not to mention his name at all. To say that he is a "good man" but "not in the running," is to condemn him to defeat in advance. The people will vote for almost anyone, even an unknown, before they will support a "sure loser." Minority and third parties seldom are able to muster their real strength on this account. The voter may believe in their principles but he is not sold on their chances.

Every candidate for public office strives to procure the endorsements of as many reputable groups and out-standing civic leaders as he can get. He always features these endorsements in his campaign literature and news releases. If he cannot win the favor of established organizations, he creates organizations of his own. They may boast a scant half dozen members but the names of the organizations are imposing. The candidate wants to create the impression that "everybody's for him." He must have a bandwagon even if it is a phony.

DOS AND DON'TS

Politics has its "dos and don'ts" the same as every other field of human activity.

Some of the Don'ts:

Don't ask questions at an opponent's meeting. He has the platform. It is his meeting.

Don't engage in fisticuffs. The voter prefers a candidate who can keep his head.

Don't advertise the other fellow's private life. The people believe that all closets, including your own, are filled with skeletons. They are not far wrong.

Don't sponsor anonymous campaign literature. The voter may be more curious about the authorship than its contents. When someone else circulates unsigned charges which should have been published in the public interest, support them bluntly. Put yourself in the author's place. The mystery of who really printed the anonymous document will be forgotten.

Don't step out of character. Be yourself.

Don't try to appear learned even if you do know a lot. The people will discover how much you know without being reminded of it.

Don't overestimate your own strength in the campaign. The political woods are filled with liars.

Don't underestimate the strength of an opponent, particularly if he is an incumbent. The "ins" nearly always develop their greatest strength in the closing days of the campaign.

Don't give a worker too much to do. He may do nothing.

Don't denounce those who have contributed to the campaign funds of the enemy unless you can make a major issue out of such contributions. You may cause them to double their contributions.

Don't organize your own political clubs in a primary campaign. In politics, people who are not "it" often sulk. Every member of your club cannot be president or secretary yet most of them will want to be. That means trouble.

Don't hand out dimes and quarters to politicians who are "broke." There are swarms of beggars in politics. They like to tell each other where the pickings are good.

Don't make promises you cannot reasonably expect to keep. Promises may win votes for you in the campaign. But the broken promise is not going to improve your chances of staying in office.

Some of the Dos:

Always keep an appointment when possible. Otherwise let your constituent know. Voters are sensitive, even about trivialities. They love attention.

Bring as much new political blood as possible into your campaign. The voters tire of the old faces.

Hard work is the best antidote for unpopularity.

Rest and reflect on the seventh day. You will wake up Monday morning with a clearer idea of what the campaign needs.

Leave the details of the campaign to your assistants. You will have done enough if you shake hands with the voters and keep your speaking engagements.

Consult often with competent observers who are not active in the campaign itself. They will have a better perspective than those who, like yourself and your managers, are so close to it.

Have frequent polls made, where possible by a professional agency. These polls will help you to keep up with the changes and trends in public sentiment.

Do as many favors for people as possible.

Preserve and index all of the records of the campaign.

Be a good sport. Politics is a game of chance.

Chapter XVIII

THE PEOPLE'S CHOICE

FOR the victorious candidate who has managed to preserve any of his conscience after the cruel exigencies of the campaign, election night has its uneasy moments.

There are telephone calls, telegrams and handshakes. The crowd cheers. The district is saved. The nation will go forward. The new hero is acclaimed. The victors collect their bets, make merry, and enjoy the celebrations.

But to you, the weary candidate-elect, all is not exhilaration and joy. Every friendly gesture is a reminder of the political debts you have accumulated. Perhaps during the campaign you have made too many promises. You may have promised the same job to more than one of your eager supporters. Maybe you made no promises at all. But Jack and Annie and Harry worked so hard! Somehow they must be rewarded.

Like the soldier who is about to go into battle, you

think of many things. Long before the campaign ended, you may have secretly wished that you had not chosen to run. You may even have hoped that you would not be elected. Inwardly, you are now conscious of the troubles you have stored up for yourself. How are you going to pay your political debts? What is to be your attitude on those controversial issues which you did not face squarely but upon which you must now take sides? Visions of questionnaires, candidates' meetings, private inquisitions, besiege your thoughts. You recall a number of very sizable contributions to your campaign fund. What price in the form of political favors must you pay for these?

It begins to dawn on you that your new public relations problems actually will grow out of the public relations program you adopted during your campaign; that your pre-election attitude is directly related to the post-election predicaments you now fear.

But the task of remaining in public office fortunately is not as difficult as the successful candidate imagines. The lessons he learned during the campaign have been invaluable. He now has his political degree; only postgraduate training is necessary to refine and add to his knowledge. He has learned the technique of electioneering. He knows what it takes to build a strong political fence. As an incumbent he knows that he will enjoy the advantages of prestige and power. He will be in the driver's seat.

On election night, however, the victorious candidate is not thinking so much about the distance he has already traveled, and the obstacles he has overcome. Amid the din and congratulations, his mind is on the hurdles he must now clear to hold fast to what he has, or to reach the next rung on the political ladder.

He sees himself on the threshold of a new political world.

Chapter XIX

PATRONAGE

Wise distribution of patronage is one of the toughest of all political jobs. It requires the most delicate public relations skill.

To the non-politically minded citizen, the endless turmoil over the division of the "spoils of office," so widely publicized in the press, merely confirms his suspicion that politics is a racket involving special favors for the few.

To the successful candidate, distribution of political patronage is a perplexing operation which involves a whole lot more than being Santa Claus to a few political pets. Indeed, the problem of satisfying his friends for services performed during the campaign, usually gives him a chronic headache and often proves to be a heart-rending task. The situation is further complicated by the real or fancied need of the victor to placate, and win the favor of, at least some of his political enemies who are in a position either to promote, or cripple, his plans.

There also is the further duty of protecting the public service. Too little competency may be as fatal to administration harmony and achievement as too much competency. The whole is what we might call a public relations sixty-four dollar question, the answer to which has not been made easier by the adoption of civil service codes. These have greatly reduced the amount of patronage to be distributed without lessening the number of applicants, each of whom imagines that he is entitled to a juicy political plum and that he is superbly qualified to handle the particular job he seeks.

NIGHTMARES OF PATRONAGE

Let us suppose that you are the newly elected governor of your State. You are sincere. You want to give the people an intelligent, efficient administration. You have a horror of public scandal. You believe in honest government. You want to be re-elected. Perhaps you have ambitions to end your political career in Washington. Instinctively you realize that much of the success of your administration will depend upon how wisely you deal with those who befriended you when you were struggling desperately to negotiate the heights, and how well you synchronize your appointive power with the legislative machinery.

You begin to soliloquize:

"Nineteen applications for bank commissioner—all

good friends—and only one can be appointed! Maybe I can tuck some of them away in other jobs. . . . No, they all want to be bank commissioner. Jim would make a good highway commissioner. Oh, I forgot, I've already promised that to Joe. There simply aren't enough jobs to go 'round. . . .

"Who can I get for beach erosion engineer? Nothing but third raters in the State. . . . There's that famous erosion engineer in the East. Maybe he would like the appointment. No, I don't dare offer it to him. The home folks won't like it. They think there's plenty of brains right here in this State. Kind of a reflection on the home talent if I go outside. . . . Well, I just won't appoint one of those third raters. Guess I'll have to lose some friends. Maybe I better talk the matter over with some of the boys. Hate to take the time, so many things to do . . . can't seem to make up my mind.

"And then there's the head of the Board of Public Affairs. That's an important job. Looks as if I've offered the job to everybody who is really competent. Nobody will accept. All getting more money than the State pays. . . . Maybe the legislature would increase the salary if I recommended it. No, that won't work. If we start raising salaries we'll have to go all the way down the line, and anyway, on second thought, the salary of members of the Board of Public Affairs is fixed in the constitution. Can't change that. Well, it looks as if I'll have to appoint some second rater. Sound second raters make pretty good public officials. . . . Sometimes the people prefer them to fellows like. . . . Too much color and mental energy. . . . No, I won't decide now. . . .

"Billy Jackson—what can I do for him . . . swell fellow . . . worked as hard as anyone in the State for me. Raised a lot of money, too. . . . Bill's competent. Too bad his reputation isn't so good. Mixed up in a few shady transactions. Maybe I could put him on the industrial commission. . . . No, he wouldn't take that. Bill won't take anything where he can't make outside deals. . . . If I don't give him what he wants, he'll be mad. Has a lot of influence with the boys in the legislature. Wonder if I could get Bill a good connection outside the administration. . . . Find a spot where he could make lots of money without embarrassing me. . . . But Bill wants to play politics. . . .

"Guess I'll go to bed and sleep on some of these things. No, I can't sleep. Too many things on my mind. There's little Joe. I've got a nice spot in mind for him, but he wants to head the motor vehicle department. Little Joe isn't big enough for that. If I offer him a smaller job, he'll get sore—think I don't appreciate his ability. Why is it so many of my friends want jobs they can't qualify for? If they'd just take a job they could fill. . . .

"Howard—now why does he want a job at all. He's got a good enough income. And my closest personal friend in some ways. No politician, didn't do a thing for me in the campaign. Just wants something that will keep him close to the governor's mansion, I guess. . . . His wife likes society and my wife won't like it if I don't give Howard a job. . . . Hate to break up a friendship that has lasted thirty years. . . .

"Got the legislature to think about, too. It's pretty evenly divided. May have trouble with my program. Guess I'll have to recognize some of the leaders. There's Senator Jones. Fought me as hard as he could. Now he's president pro tem of the Senate. Wants me to appoint Oscar Chambers to that fish and game job. Chambers was against me, too. Not very popular with the sportsmen. Only fair ability. But if I don't appoint him, Jones may throw a lot of monkey wrenches. Might wreck my legislative program. . . . Looks as if I'll have to name Chambers. A lot of my friends won't like it. . . . They'll say I'm placating my enemies. . . . No, I won't let them say that. . . . But Jones is a power. . . .

"What a mess this patronage job is. . . . Sometimes wish I hadn't been elected. . . . Oh, yes, the party chairman called me up today . . . recommended a whole flock of party workers for jobs. Never can find places for all of them He's sure getting himself in right . . . gives everybody a boost and then leaves it up to me to find the jobs. . . . Well, I've got to recognize the party. If I don't the boys will make it miserable for me when the session opens. A lot of these fellows aren't competent. Wish some one would tell me what to do. Looks as if I've got to choose a lot of incompetents or maybe lose my legislative program. . . .

"One A.M. and I haven't decided anything yet. . . . Got to get some sleep. . . . Wonder what I'm going to do about Annie. . . . Good old soul, but what a nuisance! She sure worked hard for me. You just can't keep her down. Butts into everything. A lot of women disgusted with her. . . . Awfully loyal to me, though. . . . Needs a pay check, too. . . . By God, I'm going to give old Annie a job if the whole administration goes down. I'm going to make one decision before I go to bed. Yes, I'm going to tuck Annie away in a corner of the highway commission where she can talk to herself as long and as loud as she likes. . . . Probably won't stay in her corner. I'll tell everybody just to let her spout, and pay no attention. She's a good worker and will earn her money. . . . Can't help it if she is a nuisance. She's been my friend and nobody's going to call me an ingrate!

"I suppose the boys who supported me in the primary will gripe if I appoint some of the bunch who didn't get on the bandwagon until after I was nominated. . . . Means fewer jobs for my primary friends. . . . Don't like to do it but none of us would have had jobs if a lot of folks who were against me in the primary hadn't been good sports and helped to put me over in the general election. . . . Presume I'll be misunderstood. . . .

"Now what am I going to do about Claude and Harry.
. . . Two of my best friends. Both really went to town
for me and want the same job. . . . Both of them extremely competent, too. . . . Can't seem to get either
one of them to be reasonable and agree to take something else. . . . Wonder if they would flip a coin to see
who gets the job. . . . No, each thinks I owe the place
to him. . . . Don't suppose they realize what they are
doing to me. . . .

"Two o'clock in the morning and that delegation's
going to call on me bright and early. . . . Got to get to
bed. . . . Wonder who they'll insist that I appoint as
my private secretary. . . . Can't turn them down . . .
group of party leaders, some of them my best friends.
. . . Looks like I can't refuse them. . . . My private
secretary. . . . Yes, by God, I will say no. . . . Nobody's going to pick my private secretary for me. . . .
Good thing I got married before I was elected. . . . My
friends would be here to pick my wife for me. . . .
Watch me tell 'em off. . . . Still. . . ."

NO ONE IMMUNE

If you are the mayor, supervisor, the district attorney
—or hold any office cursed with appointive powers—
you will suffer in varying degrees from the almost un-
believable embarrassments which seem to wrap themselves around every twig where a political plum is ripe
for picking. Even the fact that the office is non-partisan,

will not measurably reduce the pressure. Your party leaders still will seek preferment for those who belong to the same party as you do.

Even Presidents are not immune from the patronage germ. Washington, Jefferson, Jackson, Lincoln, Wilson, the Roosevelts and all of the others fell victim to this dread political disease. The history books record no instance where all of the members of any President's cabinet were chosen on the basis of competency alone. To a very large extent, personal friendship, party consideration, political expediency and geography, legislative harmony and many other factors entirely unrelated to that cold type of efficiency which is possible in private business, have dictated, and will continue to dictate, the choice of those whose presence in the administration generates team work.

Obviously there is no formula, no rule of thumb, which can be made to fit the intricate, delicate and widely dissimilar public relations patterns which must be cut to fit the infinite variety of patronage garments. Here case studies are of little avail. So much depends upon the personality of the administrator himself. A strong, colorful executive may find the right answers by assuming a pose or attitude which would ruin a strong, but colorless, administrator. The political situation at the moment is always one of the determining factors. When the tide is running, the administration can afford to take chances and be less considerate of both its enemies and its less desirable friends. There are times, also, when the emphasis on patronage need not be of primary concern. Perhaps some great issue has captured the public imagination. Political quarrels of the garden variety (as in 1932) are temporarily forgotten in the midst of crisis.

Some administrators make their appointments before the deluge of applications has reached their office. This method of distributing patronage at least has the merit of saving much precious time and disagreeable controversy. But it also has its drawbacks. The worker who has "gone barefooted" to help win the election feels that he has been let down when he is not even consulted. Many a political revolt has been precipitated by ignoring hard-working subordinates. There are few men in public life strong enough to overlook the wishes and feelings of their friends, and the ambitions of those whose co-operation is vital to governmental accomplishment.

KNOWING WHEN TO COMPROMISE

Up to a certain point compromises are desirable. If the parties of interest favor different applicants, harmony may often be achieved by agreeing on a third party. Every official who has to deal with a body of law makers should know how to bargain. The demands of a city councilman, State legislator or Congressman often are small. They have a friend or two from their districts whom they feel they should reward. They, too, want to be re-elected. They must "build their fences." By following their recommendations in the matter of a few minor jobs, it is often possible to win their unfaltering support for the entire administration legislative program.

Late one night, a newly elected governor was awakened to answer the call of a hill-billy legislator. This legislator insisted on seeing the governor at once. It was very important. The governor possessed an abundance of patience and he knew politicians. He had one rule, inviolate. He was never brusque with a member of the law making body, (which happened then to be in session).

"Come right out," said the governor. "I'll be glad to see you."

A few minutes later, the legislator arrived, with a dapper looking young gentleman in tow.

"Governor," said the rural representative, "my friend here wants to be bank commissioner. I understand you are going to make the appointment right soon. I know he is okay. We kinda wanted to know how we stood."

The governor had never seen nor heard of the well dressed young man.

"What are your friend's qualifications?" he parried.

The legislator thought for a moment, then replied proudly:

"Governor, he's the best *penman* you ever done see'd!"

The governor never so much as blinked. The conversation continued in a friendly manner for a few moments, then abruptly ended.

"Come to my office tomorrow afternoon and I will give you my answer," said the governor. "And say, Jim, I have some *confidential* things to talk over with you about affairs over your way."

The governor was ready with his answer when Jim arrived.

"You see," he said, "I had half way promised the banking job to someone else before I met your friend. I wish I had known about him before. A very fine and competent young man. Maybe I can do something for him later. I sure was glad you called me last night. I'd been intending right along to do something for you, Jim, but just hadn't gotten around to it. Of course I know you weren't exactly for me in the primary, but that's forgotten now. After all, we have got to think about the people first. It's up to us to make good on the legislative program we promised.

"You'll find that I always want to help the boys, too. Now you have many friends that helped you in your district. No doubt you would like to pass out a few favors in return. It just occurred to me that maybe you would like to name the oil inspector and health officer in your district. Let me know whom you want, Jim, and I'll make the appointments."

The governor made a friend out of the legislator and the legislator supported the governor's program. Public relations were improved all around. The recommendations for the two jobs weren't the best, but they were passable.

It is in this manner that administrations succeed. On two occasions important bills would have failed of passage but for this legislator's support. They were carried by a single vote!

Probably there is no phase of public relations work which requires greater self examination than the forthright handling of political pap. It's largely a matter of the individual conscience. Personality, knowledge of politicians and political ways, will ease the path but in themselves are incapable of solving the problem. Again and again the politician must choose between degrading one branch of the public service in order to improve another, or to achieve those larger things which he promised the people. Time after time, he must decide just how far he can afford to go in placating this or that element without corrupting the public service. Day after day, month after month, he must determine how much evil he will knowingly tolerate in order to save his own political hide, or how far he will dare to go in defying the will of his political friends and associates without destroying his political career.

Chapter XX

PRESSURE GROUPS

NEXT to the horde of office seekers, the so-called pressure groups are the most annoying pests with which those who manage government must contend. The number of professional lobbyists who devote their time and energies (and their clients' money) to pressure the elected representatives of the people runs into the thousands. No city hall or county court house in the nation is completely devoid of them. State capitols swarm with lobbyists during the meeting of the legislature (one of the authors, while serving in the Governor's office in Sacramento, California, a few years ago, noted that there were more lobbyists present at one special session of the legislature than there were elected State Assemblymen and Senators). No one knows exactly how many spend most of their time in Washington, D. C.

From political childhood to his political demise, the politician is obliged to deal with irate, often half-hysterical, farm, labor and business leaders, pestiferous presidents of women's organizations, noisy and boresome heads of political clubs and societies, taxpayers' associations, ministerial alliances, racial groups, nuts and screwballs—and, most potent of all—with the smooth, well-informed, well-entrenched and well-financed lobbyist of powerful business and financial groups. In short, whether candidate or office holder, the politician must continuously run the gauntlet of all of the multifarious organized cells with which the modern state is afflicted.

Describing the dilemma of the American Congressman on whom, among others, these vociferous groups descend, not every seven years like the locusts, but nearly every hour of every day, the late Raymond Clapper said:

"So he (the Congressman) has everything in one basket. His whole political future is in the hands of any organized group in his district powerful enough to cut his throat. He must yield to such groups or risk his whole public career. That places too great a strain on human nature. Men do not ordinarily go into public life for the purpose of committing political suicide."

SAYING BOTH "YES" AND "NO"

Members of legislative bodies are especially adept at inventing means of pleasing both sides to a controversy while serving only one side. A favorite trick, performed with great agility by the law maker, is to please the people by voting for a bill which he knows they want. That gives him one side. Next he quietly helps in committee to kill the appropriation without which the new measure is inoperative. Now he has won the other side. His public relations job has been expertly done. The people look at the "aye" and "no" record and applaud. Leaders of the pressure group who oppose this particular legislation see behind the curtain and chuckle to themselves.

Men have remained in public life for long numbers of years by resorting to this, and many other kinds, of political deceit. This is the seamier side to the practice of American politics. Often strong men are driven to such tactics by the fear of losing their jobs. The Socialists have a name for it—economic determinism.

There is of course that rare, forlorn and unhappy public servant who still places the general public interest above his own. He has managed somehow to get elected without specifically committing himself on an important issue. Now, he is on the spot. The time has come when he must say "yes" or "no."

What shall he do about it? How can he vote his convictions and still remain in public life?

The situation is not entirely hopeless. There are sometimes ways of helping both sides without using political sleight of hand, or raping one's conscience.

One distinguished American law maker had his own peculiar public relations formula for dealing with powerful pressure groups whose specific demands he often disapproved because he felt they did not conform to the general public interest.

When this law maker found himself invaded by a delegation representing such a group he avoided an open break by saying something like this:

"I'm sorry, gentlemen, but I cannot support your bill. I am convinced that it is not in the public interest. And I'm sure that a year or two after it is passed you will be back here asking me to help amend or repeal it. I cannot and will not vote for your measure when it comes up for passage.

"But I will do this much for you. I will help you to perfect the language of the bill so that it will be as good a bill as can be drafted from your point of view. I will try to get it out of committee for you. I will do all that I can to see that the committee approves an adequate appropriation. I will help to bring the whole matter to a vote as quickly as possible. You have a democratic right to have your bill considered on its merits. There we must part company."

Again and again this law maker rendered sincere and priceless service to pressure groups within his district, without in the least degree losing his own self respect. Again and again his predictions came true. The delegation did return to ask that the legislation either be amended or repealed. For many years this legislator commanded the respect of both sides on account of his

frankness, his abilities and his basic political integrity.
He is a highly respected private citizen at this writing—
an elder statesman in the best sense of the word.

ENLIGHTENED SELF INTEREST

In politics men lie without the semblance of reason;
dodge and duck when they might better move straight
ahead; resort to trickery when they should lay their
cards on the table, and generally conduct their public
relations on a relatively low instead of upon a high level.

This is in part the people's own fault. Politicians
gauge the voter's attitude toward different types of public conduct by the election returns. Long and bitter experience has taught them that the courageous man who
votes consistently for the general public interest is
sooner or later driven out by the demagogue who plays
the game of powerful pressure groups.

There is a saying that "bad money drives out good
money." It is equally true that bad men drive out good
men. Who else but the people are to blame?

Pressure groups undoubtedly also are responsible for
many of the bad men who drive out the good men. The
demagogue is shrewd enough to ride the pressure group
beam. Whenever we think of public relations in terms of
politics we are inevitably driven to think of how we can
improve the democratic process itself.

There is nothing inherently bad in the organization
of citizens into special groups with specific aims. It is

when these groups place their own welfare above the general public interest that they menace democratic ideals.

Good will among all the parties will continue to decline until we have public officials who will lead as well as follow; voters who will welcome and reward intelligent and courageous leadership instead of spurning and penalizing it; and pressure groups whose sponsors and adherents have learned the lesson that what is best for society as a whole will, in the long run, be best for them. Substitution of enlightened self interest for pure, unadulterated selfishness would go far toward improving the craven hypocritical and intolerable public relations which now exist between office holder and pressure group.

Chapter XXI

THE OTHER PUBLICS

No PUBLIC relations clinic for an elected public official would be complete without at least brief instruction in such routine tasks as maintaining friendly contact with his fellow politicians, the press, the party leaders, and with the people themselves.

ALWAYS PLENTY TO DO

The successful candidate is never free from campaign cares. Besides attending to his onerous official duties, he must remain on friendly terms with his fellow politicians, the newspaper fraternity, the party leaders and with all of the odd assortment of publics which comprise his constituency. Always there are political fences which need fixing as well as new fences to be built to make his future position secure. New situations are constantly arising to plague his peace of mind. Fortunate, indeed, is the elected public servant who is able to spend a quiet evening or Sabbath alone with his family.

More than any other citizen, the life of the politician is filled with ceaseless activity, petty and annoying predicaments, and recurring crises of a more serious nature. Much of the energy which he should apply to his official duties is dissipated at Sunday morning breakfasts where the politicians and party leaders gather, at noonday luncheon clubs and evening affairs where his absence would be criticized by those whose obsession is "frequent reports" from their public servants.

All of this is particularly true of those who serve the people in a local capacity.

"I don't want to go but I can't get out of it," the harassed city councilman or mayor says over and over again to himself when invited to attend a tea, a rally or some other gabfest.

Those whose official duties take them to the State and national capitols are free only in the sense that their outside activities are broadened. They do have the pleasure of looking into a new face, of shaking a different hand. But they, too, are literally smothered with demands upon their limited and precious time. Delegations of home town folks, and those who seek the coveted appointments, will travel great distances in order better to present their cases. These visitors must be welcomed and entertained.

So far as we are aware, no efficiency expert has ever

attempted to measure the time that is consumed by the average elected public servant in affairs which detract from the job he was chosen to perform. If such a survey is some day undertaken, it undoubtedly will reveal that most public officials devote more time to their public relations than they do to the immediate task at hand.

THE LITTLE CHORES

Occasionally, of course, there emerges a public figure whose interest in the legislative and administrative problems of government is so intense that he ignores nearly all of the purely political "goings on." He conserves his energy in order that he may more arduously apply himself to the research and other effort required of those who are ambitious to establish themselves as authorities in the various fields of governmental endeavor. Delegations and office seekers seldom get past his secretary.

Such "high-hatters" are not popular with the "boys." Their public relations suffer at the party confab. But if perchance the same public official finally is recognized as an outstanding and leading authority on taxes, transportation, education, the tariff, the Constitution, or on any other major subject which is in need of continuous attention, his public relations suddenly take a turn for the better.

Unfortunately, in politics, very few who are chosen have the capacity to master any complex governmental problem, no matter how much they would like to do so. Nor is this surprising, for most politicians, as we have pointed out, are peculiarly sensitive to the climate of public opinion. In our country, most successful business men pride themselves on their "practicality." They have no use for "theorists" or "intellectuals." This means, as Walter Lippmann pointed out in his *Preface to Politics* that "nothing makes them (the business men) feel so spiritually homeless as the discussion of values and an invitation to examine first principles. Ideas, most of the time, cause them genuine distress, and are as disconcerting as an idle office boy or a squawky telephone." Therefore, it is not surprising that the lesser political lights, like business men, are not theorists. They prefer to become recognized as "good fellows" who are eager and willing to do the little chores which the "big fellows," with their minds on the political cosmos, have no time for. And most of them perform the little chores well. Procuring a new light on the street intersection often is a more potent vote getter than proposing an elaborate plan of community re-development.

A Congressman once remarked to a visitor from his district:

"I suppose you wonder why I always get re-elected. After all, I'm no statesman and I know it. No important piece of legislation bears my name. None ever will. But here are some three hundred letters which came in this morning's mail, most of them containing little requests.

They will all be answered by tonight. In this office we know how to satisfy these little requests quickly. We have friends in every government department who are glad to oblige promptly with the information we want. As a result, we have thousands of friends among the 'little folks' back home, people you never even hear about. When it comes to voting on important legislation, I take the word of others who know what it's all about and whose position is pretty apt to be in accord with the wishes of the people in my district. My formula has worked. I leave the thinking to others, and do these little things myself. I get $10,000 a year for being a good chore boy. I think the people are getting value received. Evidently they think so, too."

This Congressman was elected for ten successive terms; then a sudden political tide terminated his career as an errand runner.

THE NEWSPAPERMEN KNOW

Perhaps as good a way as any to take the mental measure of an elected public servant is to observe how much time he has for these minor public relations activities, which, cumulatively, are so vital to so many of those in public life who could not otherwise survive. But even these feverish little activities may be over-done. Familiarity breeds contempt, people weary of the same old face, the same old stuff. Gradually, it dawns upon them that their chore boy is indeed a chore boy, nothing else.

In short, an elected official probably will establish the most enduring public relations with his constituents if he gets around just enough to make them wish they could see him more often. Even the busy statesman can and should take out enough time for this. The people know that he is busy and will be satisfied with an occasional appearance. The public relations problem of those who have less to occupy their attention is not dissimilar. It is very simple to create the illusion that you are busier than you really are. Fairly frequent appearances will be sufficient to satisfy your constituency. It is always well to suggest that you would be delighted to show yourself more often but that "heavy affairs of state" forbid. The people are slow to distinguish between the great and the "near great."

The newspaper men are not so slow in drawing this distinction. They can spot a political phony as easily as they can detect the smell of bath-tub gin. They are not fond of either. The easiest way for a public official to get along with members of the Fourth Estate is to stay in character.

Newspapermen who do the political beat usually turn cynical. They understand all about "build-ups." They are in the build-up business. And they are equally well acquainted with the art of puncturing a badly inflated political balloon. They know both how to create and destroy. It pays to be frank with them. If you are a "little shot," it is well to suggest that you are "only a country boy trying to get along in the big city." Any little help will be appreciated. You don't expect much. Perhaps they would be kind enough to mention your name, or not take a poke at you.

Reporters like to be "in on the know." It helps with the city editor for them to be able to whisper that a good story is about to break, and that they have all the low-down. Papers have deadlines. If the reporter knows in advance what is about to happen, and why, he can have much of his copy ready. He need only write his lead when the story is released. Up-to-the-minute news is the principal commodity in which the reporter deals. He will not knowingly violate a confidence. Often a confidential tip-off will spare you grief. There are very few political secrets which reporters do not learn. They are experts at putting two and two together. A "rumor story" may destroy the effect of the real story. They will not publish anything if you have given them the "inside." The real story will be the first story to break.

Ask the newsman's advice when you are on the spot. It will please him. And he may give you the clue to the best way out of your dilemma. He knows politics and politicians as well, if not better, than you do unless you are an old hand at the game. He has his secrets, too. It will pay you to find out what these are. He will tell you if he trusts and likes you.

Do not treat the reporter as an enemy merely because his paper is opposing you, nor make it difficult for him to secure the facts about general news items. If you must now and then favor the paper that is favoring you, he will understand. Tell him that you are sorry. Make him feel that he is a person apart from his paper. Never rib him. It is well to remember that he always has the last word, that you can fight and beat a publisher, but that you can't fight and beat a reporter; that you can overcome the effect of a nasty editorial (which few people probably have read), but that you cannot parry a wallop handed you in the news column which nearly everyone has read.

"BUILD" YOUR FRIENDS

Dealing with your fellow politician and the party leaders involves quite a different technique. Here the problem in public relations is to tell the politician and party leader as little as possible, without offending him. Politicians and party leaders do not keep secrets. They broadcast them! What these likable busybodies really want is recognition for themselves—a place in the sun. The simplest way to hold their friendship is to pass the honors around—make "big shots" out of them.

If you are a city councilman, let someone else be county chairman. If a political rally is scheduled, let some deserving friend preside at the meeting. Hogging the show is not conducive to good public relations, though a surprisingly large number get away with it in politics. Finally, however, the worm usually turns. If you need and want valuable and loyal friends, they must be recognized, encouraged, built up. The more generous you are in sharing the honors and the credit of political life, the less apt you are to have serious opposition, at least within your own ranks, when election year rolls around. The more selfish you are, the more likely that opposition among your erstwhile friends will develop and crystallize behind a formidable opponent.

YOU MUST GET ALONG WITH PEOPLE

In politics, the homely virtues do count. It is hard to defeat common honesty, candor, tolerance and good morals where these are coupled with reasonable intelligence, a pleasing personality, modest resources and a favorable political situation.

And, if the fates have been kind, and you have become the people's choice, it is well to remember the success formula of the Negro preacher. Describing his method of pleasing his congregation, he said: "I jes makes it a point to co-operate wid de inevidable!"

It may not always be statesmanlike to "co-operate wid de inevidable," but the elected official will always find it prudent not to fight against the inevitable.

Chapter XXII

POLITICAL MORALS AND ETHICS

THERE is an unfortunate barrier between the people and the politician. On the one hand, this barrier is the people's inherent mistrust of the politician; on the other, it is the politician's constitutional fear of the voter. The issue simmers down to one of morals and ethics.

The history of American politics—municipal, State and national—is repleat with stories of high-minded, energetic, sincere men and women who have sacrificed private careers and fortune to bring about much needed reforms or to oust corrupt or incompetent officials. Too often, unfortunately, these worthy reformers have met with a stony silence from the voters, or what is even worse, the wise and indulgent smile of an electorate which didn't give a damn. These are the heartbreaking episodes which turn reformers into cynics and make them easy prey for the special interests out to mulct the public.

Each passing year produces a large crop of political neophytes, eager to do good for the city, State or country, who believe that the only essential to success at the polls is to present "the true facts" to the electorate. And year after year the great majority of these political freshmen are snowed under on election day. What they have failed to realize—over and above the techniques of public relations discussed in preceding chapters—is that while facts or good logic may win in a debating society they do not always win in politics. The successful politician must deal with the hopes and visions, the will and desire—or (as it is called in political science) the dynamics of men.

The able politician accepts man as he is—not as he ought to be—and builds upon that basis. To maintain his own integrity he refuses to be a mere mouthpiece for his constituent's whims or prejudices. On the other hand, he does not try to move too far in front of them, for he knows that a general is of little use unless he has an army. The public official, like the military officer, who loses contact with his own forces, will soon be out of business.

The standard of public relations in politics will improve in exact proportion as these mistrusts are eliminated and as mutual confidence between the people and the politician is created.

There is never likely to be an effective, voluntarily established code of morals and ethics for politicians— any Ten Commandments, neatly framed, to decorate his office wall, constantly there to remind him that the game has certain rules which he is honor bound to obey.

Such codes have done much good, particularly in the recognized professions, where they can be reasonably enforced. But the politician remains a free lance. Either he has a sense of public morals and ethics, or he has not. If he is instinctively decent, no code is necessary. If he is a rogue, no code will bind him. He has none of the pride of the professional man in his profession, none of the pride of the business man in his trade association.

If the politician were provided with a code, he could break it with impunity. He would not face "disbarment." Under our democratic system no experience, no educational, moral or other qualifications can logically be required of the candidate who is about to throw his hat in the ring, or of the ward heeler or party leader who aids in his election. The mere right to vote, arbitrarily fixed by law, is sufficient to qualify any citizen to practice politics, either as a full or part time calling.

In the past, mistrust by the people of all politicians, good or bad, has, in fact, constituted the only effective control which the voter exercises over those who manage politics and government.

"Thus far shalt thou go and no farther!" These are

words which every politician has learned to fear. He knows that there is a limit to what the people will endure. He may be able to manipulate juries and judges but when the people have spoken through the ballot box, he knows that the verdict is final. There is no appeal from the decisions of the court of public opinion.

But if the people have good reason to mistrust the politician, so they have still more urgent reason to make his lot easier. Good morals and high ethical standards cannot be divorced from environment and economic status. There is no field of human endeavor where the competition is fiercer, or where the struggle for survival is more desperate, than in the political arena.

Most of the rewards are small, unbelievably meager for the tremendous effort that must be expended to win and to hold them. Every step up the political ladder involves another grueling struggle. For the politician, every election day is another doomsday.

The voter is a hard employer, a cruel task maker. He pays low wages, provides no fair and orderly system of promotion for services well performed. His pet servant today is his pet aversion tomorrow. In such circumstances, men's minds do not dwell on morals and ethics. Few there are in public life who are able to survive the battle for political preferment with their morals and ethics intact.

It is seldom indeed that the elected politician—even

if he is crooked—makes a fortune out of his shady dealings. The Tweeds and Pendergasts are rare birds in the political aviary.

The people who really profit are the political bosses who hold no, or only minor, elective offices, as well as the "respectable" lawyers, bankers, railroad, shipping, utility and other business magnates, whose bribery or blackmail have turned spineless, cynical or money-hungry public servants into instruments of corruption.

Unfortunately, the public itself has too frequently acquiesced in the idea that looting the public coffer is not a crime. Indicative of this attitude was the debate between two candidates for a high public office in which one of them said: "I admit that the elected representatives of my party have too often dipped their fingers into the public till, but whenever the representatives of my opponent's party have been in office, they have not been satisfied with such petty pilfering. They have carried off the cash box."

In these pages we have sought faithfully to describe the problems of the politician, and how he meets them. The reader must judge for himself how well the morals and ethics of those who take an active interest in public life compare with those who prefer to remain apart from the activities which contribute either to the success or failure of the democratic way.

In comparing the morals and ethics of the politician with the standards that exist in business and the professions, one should not make a one-sided decision. In the realm of private endeavor, there is room for criticism, too. Business and the professions are not lily white any more than politics is without its streaks of black. Men chisel to get votes but men also plan unfair ways to win markets and to convince juries.

At the bottom of nearly all scandals in public life we find the crooked politician plus either the crooked business man, crooked lawyer, crooked labor racketeer, or others whose loyalty to democratic ideals and feeling for the moral and ethical rules of life are ignored whenever they believe that their own interests can better be served by less idealistic considerations.

Trust—not distrust—is the basis of all sound public relations, whether in public or private life. Not until the politician has been given a chance to live and to function like all other citizens, will he begin to think in terms of morals and ethics. Not until politics has been given the dignity of the cloth and the worthy politician is properly respected will the intelligent and ambitious youth of tomorrow toss his hat in the ring, and enlist for life in the peace time services of his country.

Theodore Roosevelt had a long and distinguished career as a public servant; and during that period he set and discarded various standards for himself. At one time, for example, he favored a policy of compromise between principles and political expediency, but found that this became too tortuous a task. Finally he evolved the following rule of conduct: Approach the tasks you have to fulfill as though the office you now hold were the last and highest you will ever have, bearing in mind that you want to leave that office with a clear conscience and a feeling of a job well done.

All of us know that every war President has been given great powers by Congress—powers which could easily be used to suppress criticism of opponents.

Among the many bitter critics of President Wilson in the period immediately preceding our entry into World War I, none was so vicious as the Hearst press and its able editorial columnist, Arthur Brisbane.

Immediately after America's entry into the war, Mr. Brisbane, fearful that the proposed Espionage Act might be used to force him to desist in these attacks upon the President, wrote a letter to Woodrow Wilson asking if the chief executive intended to use the new powers to be conferred upon him by the proposed law to shield himself against criticism. President Wilson's letter dated April 27, 1917 follows:

"My dear Mr. Brisbane:

"I sincerely appreciate the frankness of your interesting letter of April 20, with reference to the so-called Espionage Bill now awaiting the action of Congress. I approve of this legislation, but I need not assure you and those interested in it, that, whatever action Congress may decide upon, so far as I am personally concerned, I shall not apply or permit any part of this law to apply to me or any of my official acts, or in any way to be used as a shield against criticism.

"I can imagine no greater disservice to the country than to establish a system of censorship that would deny to the people of a free republic like our own their indisputable right to criticise their own public officials. While exercising the powers of the office I hold, I would regret in a crisis like the one through which we are passing to lose the benefit of patriotic and intelligent criticism.

"In these trying times, one can feel certain only of his motives, which he must strive to purge of selfishness of every kind, and wait with patience for the judgment of a calmer day to vindicate the wisdom of the course he has tried conscientiously to follow. Thank you for having written me.

"Cordially and sincerely yours,
"Woodrow Wilson."

High moral and ethical standards have their roots in the souls of men. Men's souls become hardened and calloused when fed upon mistrust and abuse. The politician is of the people. There need be no worry about his morals and ethics when the morals and ethics of the peo-

ple themselves are entitled to praise. The chief concern
of those engaged in the public relations of politics is
nothing less than lifting the whole of society onto a
higher and a more civilized plateau.

That is the task of every citizen of the democracy.